With the London Regiment in the Middle East, 1917

London Men in Palestine

With the London Regiment in the Middle East, 1917

Accounts of the 60th Division During the
Palestine Campaign in the First World War

ILLUSTRATED

London Men in Palestine

Rowlands Coldicott

The Taking of Jerusalem

Edmund Dane

LEONAUR

With the London Regiment in the Middle East, 1917
Accounts of the 60th Division During the Palestine Campaign in the First World War
London Men in Palestine
by Rowlands Coldicott
The Taking of Jerusalem
by Edmund Dane

ILLUSTRATED

FIRST EDITION

Leonaur is an imprint of Oakpast Ltd
Copyright in this form © 2021 Oakpast Ltd

ISBN: 978-1-915234-30-8 (hardcover)
ISBN: 978-1-915234-31-5 (softcover)

http://www.leonaur.com

Publisher's Notes

Contents

DEDICATION

TO THE EGYPTIAN EXPEDITIONARY FORCE

The past's the past, when all is said,
Better, perhaps, to let things be;
For all our art, the dead are dead,
Even the men were phantasy;
They gossiped blithely, past belief,
Beyond the granted moment stayed,
Marched in the daylight, ate their beef,
And now, behold, they fade.

But you, the living—you, glad hearts,
Who by adventure recognise
In this past-haunting book the parts
You played out once, 'neath other skies,
For you, and for that greater throng,
For all who trod the Road of Wire,
Heroes unchronicled in song,
Trembling, I sweep the lyre.

Another Spring, and you'll forget
The songs you sang, the foreign scene,
Urchins that chorused "cig-ar-ette,"
Vendors of melons "veery clean,"
Kantara and its myriad tents,
Cairo, the Sphinx and all the sights.
The low bazaar, the acrid scents,
The silvern Eastern nights.

There's plenty left to write about,
A hundred songs are held in leash;
Are there no tales of Tank redoubt,
Can no one sing of El Arish?

7

When will the Katia tale be told?
Or that concealed disastrous fight
At Gaza, when the troops were sold
By one who counselled flight?

Those early days! and now long trains,
Luxuriously filled, ride
Without a tremor through the plains
By Belah, Gaza, Deir Sineid;
While in the desert, ashen-grey,
Beneath the moon, deserted, stand
Old block-houses, and day by day
The trenches fill with sand.

Egypt, to you our bitter strife
A quarrel of small children seems;
You and your tranquil Delta-life
Are plunged, as ever, in dim dreams.
Protected! Conquered! Who'll divine
What future peoples here shall bleed
Or come to govern Palestine?
How wrong despatches read!

Shut in thy pulseless bosom of stone,
Committed to thy shifting dunes,
The seeds, the sowers, and the sown,
Our deepest thoughts, our lightest tunes,
Our desert camps, our desert fights,
Our conquest of Jerusalem,
You take them 'neath the moon o'nights,
And, silent, bury them.

Preface

This book has been written in many places, most of it during the closing scenes of the war. Vaguely conceived in Egypt, but not getting any further than the title, it was begun one morning at Cambridge in the house of a friend. I was telling my hostess some of my adventures in Palestine, when the title of the projected book suddenly popped out. "Sit down at once and begin it," she said, "here, in this room." What could a guest do but obey? And so, the ice was broken, and the company and I set out once more upon our adventures. A tent on the East coast and the approach of winter saw, in a period of wet weather that came too early to inspire the chapter about the rains, the completion of the first pages.

A halcyon interlude in a Sussex cottage, for which I render grateful thanks to the Eastern Command, helped it along. At Fourth Army Headquarters, France, I left the dusty plains of Philistia and came to the foot of the Judaean hills. The armistice found my body in Belgium, my spirit on the Jerusalem road. Then came a three months' slump, shepherding the German hosts to the Rhine. Blessed demobilisation reopened the door of the Sussex cottage. A month flew by, and lo! a volume.

Whatever may be said by that other division, those gallant fellows who first forced the approaches and sat down on Nebi Samvil and neighbouring barren heights, it was the London men who took Jerusalem, an achievement history will not be able to blink at or forget. The drums and tramplings of more than three conquests have passed over the city since Titus embattled his legions against it, but no man has ever dreamed that it was destined to be stormed again, on a misty December morning, by the trained-band captains of famous London Town. One of these, in no spirit of pride or foolish partisan rejoicing, but glad to be alive and to have the tale to tell, now delivers to friends and strangers this crowning adventure.

The myriad names from France that wait the histories of the future have a confused splendour that dazzles those who seek to distinguish them and assign to each its tale; but the taking of Jerusalem, inferior as a spectacle of brute energy, and hardly illustrating at all the more devilish developments of modern warfare, can be shown in a clear, hard light, historically and romantically the greatest of all the episodes that have flamed on a sudden into public view out of the less regarded spaces of the war. Beersheba stood prologue to the brilliant tale whose climax of rain, misery, glory and triumphant progress these pages hope to keep fresh for the years to come.

And yet the story is conceived on humble, almost personal lines. You will not find in this book the full-fig military narrative; comments upon strategy, divisions rehandled in words, talk of the characteristics of a general. The net of prose is set in sight of smaller birds; chiefly a mass of private sorrows and rejoicings are entangled here. Out of a number of personal narratives of this kind some ultimate history of the war perhaps may be compiled. The story of how men of the greatest city of the modern world came to take the most renowned city of all time will be one of its romantic pages.

My labour has been given mainly to recording something of the strain, urgency, and bodily feeling of our marchings in Philistia and advance to Jerusalem. If truth of atmosphere is held to inhabit these pages, that labour has not been in vain. It is an effort of memory, supported by that famous map, "Sheet Seventeen." Doubtless she has played some pranks with me—a tree, the configuration of a mass of rock, even a village may be wrongfully described or put out of due sequence. I hope those who know will write long and interesting letters, setting me right. But the pain, the weariness, the inner life: I could not go wrong there.

Rowlands Coldicott.

Middleton-on-Sea
Sussex
October, 1919.

CHAPTER 1

After Sheria

1: WE GO TO HUJ

Packs on. The two magic words, like the whip of an overseer, stung the column into life. It was the end of the first ten minutes' halt, at the outset of a march that had something of a triumphant progress in it, something of a pursuit. Sheria lay behind us. The men, sun-tired and battle-tired, dusty little chaps clad simply in shorts and shirts and almost eclipsed under their yellow pith helmets, had to reconquer themselves smartly in order to come to heel. They were very weary. The confused battle of yesterday, begun half blindly at the first glimmering of dawn, itself sequent to another engagement and another pursuit, had, with the heat, and the flies, and the lack of water, dulled a little an exultant sense of victory. We had at first supposed that the campaign, brilliantly begun at Beersheba, would by this time have been nearly over.

Now it was opening out unimagined *vistas*. The capture of Sheria's well-springs and the huge dumps that lay behind them had, with the almost simultaneous crash and ruin of Gaza, freed our army for adventures no one had contemplated. These early days of November were finding us nearly upon a line that might, it had been suggested, be won by January. The programme had been overrun; everything was possible; everyone had caught the infection: we were exalted, but our bodies were sickly tired.

Slowly the men picked up their equipment, masses of inert weight, shoved half-eaten biscuits into their pockets, and fell in. Breakfast had been a failure that morning. A sudden order to follow up the cavalry had taken us, in the act of distributing rations, straight from yesterday's battle positions. Half-emptied cases of bully-beef, the end of a

SKETCH·MAP·SHOWING THE LONDONERS'

MEDITERRANEAN SEA

Jaffa Trailw.

El Mesmiye

Esdud

El Kustine

Wadi Mesza

Askalon

El Mejdele

Narrow Gauge Railway

Deir Sineid

Wadi Hesy

Jemmameh

Beit Hanun

Hlij

GAZA

Ali-el Muntar

Sheikh Abbas

Tel-el Jemme

Wadi Ghuzze

Wadi-esh-Sheria

SHERIA WELLS

Shellal

Tel-el Fara

Karim

BEERSHEBA

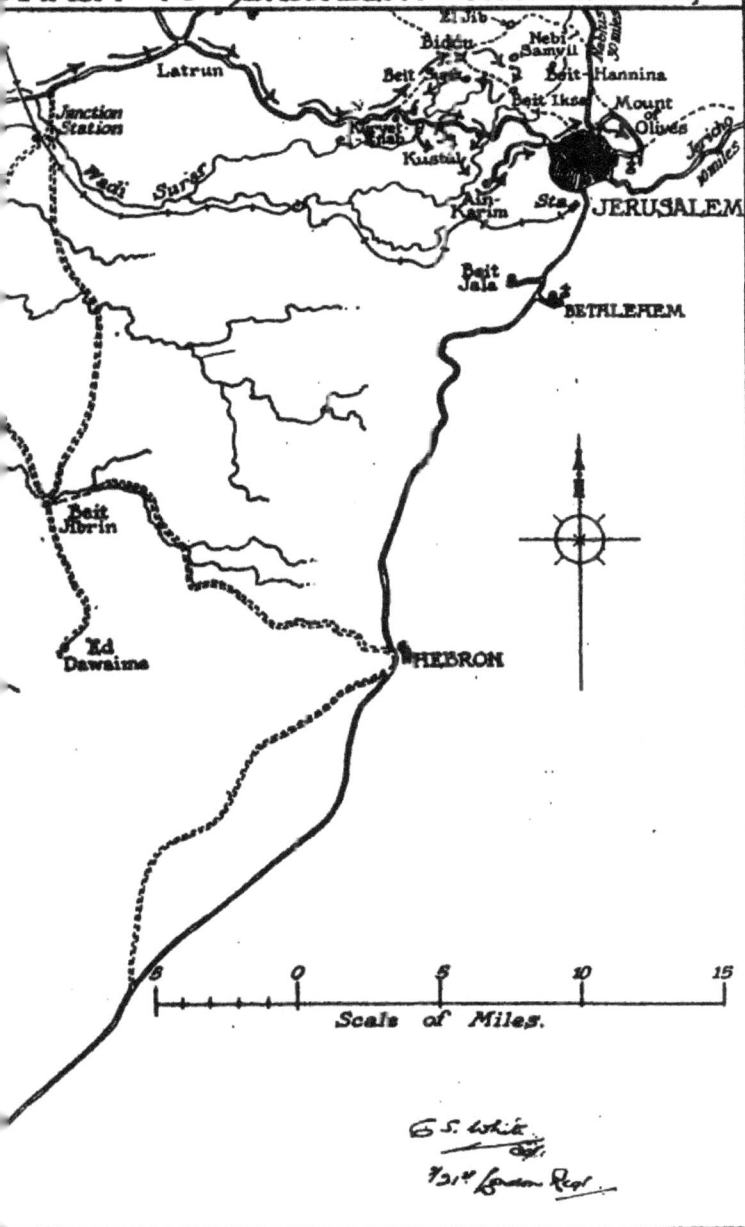

MARCH · TO · JERUSALEM ~ NOV · DEC · 1917:

sackful of sugar, a tin of biscuits, all regretfully abandoned, spoke the urgency of our departure. Yesterday we had been contesting, yard by yard, for the possession of these rolling plains; in the afternoon cavalry had swept through our thin forward fringe, and the fight was over. Dusk had found us wearily planting battle-outposts against the Turks' possible return. But the work of harrying him out of the great cracks or clefts in the dirt plain that go by the name of *wadis* had been well done. He would not trouble Sheria again.

Sheria, Gaza, and a small place named Huj form the eastern, western, and northern points respectively of a squat triangle whose base measures fifteen miles. These places lie in a series of expanses of bare brown earth divided irregularly by *wadis* widely differing in character and extent. Sometimes you do not see them until you come to their very edge, when a narrow but deep fissure, all hard earth, appears, with the dried carcase of a goat, perhaps, lying in its fantastic bottom.

Yet amid these obstacles a column may press its way if it proceed northwesterly, and a fairly continuous terrain exists to Huj, which, the map told us, was some two hundred feet lower than the ground we now tramped, clear of the north-flung tentacles of the great Wadi Sheria the march seemed tediously straight, and in the hour-long non-appearance of even a sign of the place towards which we were making, endless.

Monotony is the keyword to reopen the gates that have swung to upon that daylong march, the monotony of toilsome pursuit. The expanses of earth everywhere around us, slightly rising or slightly falling, the thin lip of a *wadi*-end passed to the right or left, a few scattered objects, packs, stretchers, gas-masks, dropped by the enemy in his flight, did not give much to occupy the mind. The cloudless sky we had lived under so long gave not the slightest sign of the rains authority warned us were at hand. From the blazing sun no one could for a moment hide. My mare, an ungainly but hardy animal who had served me well in France and Macedonia, provided at halts the only exception, a patch (when she could be persuaded to stand still) of splendid black shade.

The strictly punctual recurrence of the halts, little medical teaspoonfuls of rest taken by the rank and file with a studied quietness that hinted past experiences, formed, with the agony of the intervening hours, a human monotony that chimed with the landscape. And yet all this was triumphed over and quashed by our consciousness of the spectacle we in the aggregate afforded; surely a fit subject for historians to come. A mass of soldiery, battalion in line with battalion, the wing of an army, moving intact with ambulances, guns, and that body of miscellaneous transport Eastern conditions require, protected by cavalry operating beyond the horizon—this gave room for spacious thoughts, letting us know the import of our dramatic act. Never in a long experience of marches can I remember one so monotonous, or so well supported by the unconscious moral aid lent by each individual to the mass.

And now the day was half over, and higher ground enabled us to see in the far distance over our left shoulder trees and a mass of buildings. Speculation ran down the ranks as to whether that was Gaza, and my map confirmed it. Through glasses I took a long look at the town we had heard so much of but had never seen. The corps that knew it too well had already left it behind, and were pushing vigorously on, astride the railway. We never guessed that we too were destined in a few days to harbour in front of its defences.

As the afternoon wore on everyone became more inclined to silence. Conversation was at last almost limited to oaths and the successive discovery by eager fanatics of features in the country in front of us that must, they said, be Huj. Then as we drew near to each imagined site, a tree or two perhaps or a ruined building, and continued to march on, and through, and beyond, deeper shades of despair descended upon the toiling company. The supremely inapposite remark called out suddenly by the licensed wag met with, for once, no audience. The uplift provided for the first few hours by the spectacular nature of the show had worn itself out now, as things of that nature will, and the men had to rely, as ever in the long run, upon moral qualities.

But the fact that we had passed trees, and the gradually changing nature of the ground, actually becoming green, showed that we were on the slightly lower country among whose low hill-lands Huj was supposed to be. Evidently at some time of the year this place had been of a certain dampness, and could still support life on the remembrance. We wound to the left, and then on a sudden were upon, not Huj, but, in some tumbled ground that defended it, a wrecked enemy battery.

In Palestine darkness comes with quick strides, and twilight is of almost no duration; yet the brief minutes the country allows you are magic ones, when the sun's failing light brings out warm browns and wonderful russets among which people stand or move, like figures in a painted book. Within the narrow compass of this charmed period, ourselves a moving pageant, we now beheld the results of a conflict of the utmost violence: a battery charged by the Warwicks and the Worcesters and put to the sword. The guns, laid that afternoon in our direction, were now thrown this way and that by the shock of impact and the Turks' last desperate attempts to get away. Equipment, lanterns, and mess stores lay upon the ground; dead men and horses covered with dust and blood sprawled to the left and right.

In a Turkish ambulance wagon bandaged Turks were groaning. A few files of ragged and dusty prisoners, clad in the odds and ends of many uniforms, shuffled away as we passed, and I noted in their rear a little family party, a Turkish doctor with his fair Circassian wife, a baby in her arms. What first memories for a child!

Consumed with interest at the sight of all this, trying to get it into my brain, now by fixing particular objects, now by taking comprehensive looks, I rode at the head of the old company piloted safely for so many months in so many regions. "Marie Lloyd," my mare, who sniffed and sidled a little as her nostrils warned her of the dead animals, was as weary as the men, who now, in spite of their surroundings, began to lag. Thinking of what in ten minutes' time we should all be desiring, I pointed out to the sergeant-major various wooden articles we could send men back for, and smash up, and burn.

In a minute or so we had passed the wreckage, and the guns lay behind us. We were winding amongst the hillocks, and I began to fear I should not be able to find the place again in the darkness. The men now needed exhorting, but no cheery syllables announcing the end of the march could rouse more than the thinnest response.

"Where am I to go?" I asked the adjutant, who stood grimly watching us, allotting, I supposed, in the absence of an advance officer, each company its portion of land.

"Anywhere here," he answered, with a nod over his shoulder; "the men will have to lie down for a bit before you do anything."

"Any water?" This in a whisper.

"Don't think so. The battalion's frightfully short. I'll try and send you along two *fanatic*, (small portable water-tanks of tinned copper) I hope to God the camels will find the way here tonight. The real trouble's our transport. Hoyle says the horses can't move tomorrow without a drink."

The platoons, almost automatically, formed close column and stood hunched up waiting the word to lie down, which came from the very bottom of my heart. Domestic labours were in front of us, but nothing mattered now that we had arrived. Slinging off my equip-

"Over the bare and trackless plain"

ment, I called up the subalterns.

"Trobus, cut along to B.H.Q. and see what water they are going to let us have. Mac said two *fanatis*. Try to get three. Temple, find out when and where quartermaster is issuing rations, and let me know. Jackson, I want you to get some food for ourselves, get our bivvies up, and look after the servants. Quite clear? Right-ho! Come along, sergeant-major, get the sanitary men and we'll go and site the latrines. You know what the men are. Animals. Bring a torch. Over there, I think. Every man in the company must be told."

To the accompaniment of these labours night, closed upon Huj.

2: The Wells of Jemmameh

"Jemimer" is what we called it, with our Cockney irreverence for foreign names, and, like most places in Palestine where water is, it took a deal of getting to. The major, who on a fairly fit horse had done a short early-morning one-man reconnaissance, reported that it was downhill all the way, and gave us the impression that it lay just round the corner. Glutted with captured Turkish bread and well filled up with sticky dates, we set out in high hopes, eager to arrive at the ancient watering-place and forget in plenty the painful difficulties and anxieties of the last two days.

The Huj bivouac ground had quickly become noisome, for dead horses in hot countries very soon begin to tell you that they are unburied. A few spadefuls of earth had turned each animal into an unsightly dusty hillock, through which a leg or nasty muzzle protruded, to remind us, if need be, that they were not natural features of the landscape. Water had been the dominant theme, the shortage of it, the need of it, and how best and quickest to decant it from the *fanatis* into the men's bottles without losing a drop.

Nobody had been able to wash properly after the march from Sheria; the rest had been really only a temporary respite from the fatigue of moving on. The animals, many hours without water on their arrival, had been taken during the night in search of it by the transport men, who had returned after a nine miles' trek to report that the troughs were monopolised entirely by the cavalry, and that sheer lack of space made the watering of ours in that direction impracticable.

Finally, a way out had been found, but most of the chargers were dangerously weak and could not be ridden. Hoyle, whose fiery energy had accomplished so much for us since our departure, only ten days ago, from a far-off barren bump beside the Wadi Ghuzze known as Tel

El Fara, had been vehement that morning at headquarters on the impossibility of urging the beasts further if water and some rest for them could not presently be got. "It can't be done," he said, meaning that if it were possible it would be accomplished, and he would do it. Native of an ancient troubled kingdom, he spoke the "a" short in this general answer of his to officers who came bothering for extra transport. You left his lines with a flea in your ear, but the mule you asked for usually appeared at the crisis.

It was on the tongue of everyone that rest and peace awaited us at this garden of wells that lay so luckily within an easy march. There we were to stop and recover ourselves while the enemy, who had retreated into the unknown, would be harried we hoped by the cavalry, a job to their mind. We had had enough of slaughter. Our hatred of the Turk had evaporated after he had turned tail, and our thoughts, moving for a while in areas of speculation, had returned to their usual pasturage—the fields of food and drink. The romantic tale, if you come to close quarters with it, is very different from the troubadour's song-story or the series of select episodes that become the epic.

The most exalted warriors must eat and drink, and they spend much of their time doing it, removing the traces of it, or forecasting amongst themselves when and where the next meal will be. Add to this some humbler domestic necessities and the getting of a little sleep, and your warrior's day is full. His talk is of these elementary topics, his sleep often more dreamless than a dog's. In the ranks under a full pack, he stumbles on much like a laden animal, his mind absorbed in the same vague feeling towards a goal. I paint the normal here. He is also, Heaven be praised, upon occasion, a generating-point for enthusiasm, an instrument to be played upon, a reservoir of effort whose capacity can never be gauged.

Tranquillity was in the ascendant as the companies tailed off in turn from close column and headed away, each with its train of mules. We had been good boys that morning. The late start—it was nearly ten o'clock—had allowed us to clean up our camping grounds with unusual care, and long before the time published in orders, men and officers could be seen lying on the ground beside rows of neatly arranged packs, talking, smoking, or dozing, business done.

No officers' mess cook struggled on the ground beside a basket bulging with jumbled packages while an angry mess president told him to get a move on and the damned thing done up somehow. Company commanders had strolled over towards each other and exchanged sweet nothings, unusual unbendings for such jealously competing tyrants. Even the colonel cursed not, and the brow of the adjutant was clear.

A few hundred yards, and we were quit of the slightly tumbled ground where we had bivouacked, and trod open country. Now we were crossing a great bare earthen expanse littered with odds and ends of Turkish rubbish, packs, and the black enamelled metal cases in which German gas-helmets are carried. This Turkish Army, considering it was in retreat, had not left much behind it, but the men had certainly taken the opportunity to rid themselves of their gas-respirators. To our left, in the distance, lay what we imagined was Huj, but we could see little except an enormous dump of timber—a splendid haul for our R.E.'s in a land where almost all timber is imported—one or two trucks, and the hangar of an aerodrome.

We marched on, halted, as usual, at ten minutes to the clock hour, and soon afterwards passed through a village, the first buildings many of us had seen since we left Beersheba. It seemed to be rather tumbledown or else knocked about—it is sometimes difficult to tell which in the East; and it was mud-coloured and very old, but with a wooden door or two about it and beams of wood here and there which we looked at greedily as we passed. A few men, probably of another corps, were occupied on some business there, mending a wrecked well-gear, I fancy, and we thought how lucky those fellows were, for they would have a fire to sit round that night, and perhaps four walls within which to sleep. Such luck never came our way. Still, we were going to the wells.

After we left the village the country became more arid and the dust more stifling. We had been very gradually descending for some time, and were now approaching a barren district pierced in all directions by a *wadi* whose main bed we presently crossed. Down the slight bank—for it was a shallow, open, flat one—we broke our choking way, stumbled over the central bed of loose white pebbles, and scrambled up and out on to a second desert of dust less deeply broken.

The route was marked depressingly by the bodies of horses who had fallen exhausted, and by the ribs of camels overcome in a more distant past. Obviously, this march had tried to the utmost earlier adventurers than ourselves. The pace began to slacken, the weaker men to show signs of great fatigue. Gradually during the past two hours we had come to realise that the easy march promised us by the major was a misconception, and bitter indeed were the comments bandied about on this subject by rank and file.

"Where my caravan has rested—God! I wish we could."

"Look at that old horse. Bill, that's what you'll look like one of these days."

"Shut up, you, what's the good of being cheerful?"

"What'll anybody give for my dates? Will exchange for pot of beer or anything useful."

"I like these nice little easy marches, down the hill and round the corner. What?"

"D'you remember that day we come from that place by the railway and took over by night from those chaps on the plain? Funny lot of blighters they were. Didn't know nothing about anything, and weren't they in a hell of a hurry to clear out. Gawd, what a march that was!"

"Ain't so easy as this is going to be, looking for these bloody wells."

"Look at the captain's horse; she won't go much further."

The track doubled, twisted, and led us across an open expanse into the *wadi* again. Another extra-special dose of dust, and increased thirst for the men, who were afraid to touch their water-bottles, knowing that even at the end of a march when water is promised it does not always come. Again, the track went off at a bend, and for the third time this infernal *wadi* flung its yellow body disobligingly in our way. This time we crossed it in silence. Then the track straightened out.

Halts come on marches at ten minutes to the clock hour. A matter of the strictest routine, this observance is not altered or broken into except when direst necessity compels. The march then becomes a "forced march," time being gained not by quickening pace, but by drawing upon these intervals of rest. For soldiers, therefore, marches are normally divided into an indefinite number of periods of fifty minutes each, rounded by a ten minutes' halt. How eagerly are those halts looked for! With what new struggling resolves wearily left behind!

The heat was now sweltering, the dust powdered us grey, the element of torture in the march swiftly became dominant. Now began a time when every man in the company required watching and the unobtrusive supervision by the officers grew lynx-like. There were certain known men, we knew, who would have to throw their very best into the struggle in order to hold out. There were others whose weak moral fibre would cause them, if they were not shamed and exhorted out of it, pitifully to succumb.

And there were many, going to an undecorated death, nameless aristocrats of London shops and offices, magnificent in their high hearts as those nobles of France whose calm, invincible demeanour won, in the Revolution, the admiration of all Europe. Beyond the praises of poets, the sublime, silent endurance of these men, whose quiet suffering escapes the trick of a phrase or the rhythmic beat of a line, and made their officers feel at the time unworthy to be set over them, to order them about or blame. They seemed to have something stronger than strength to rely on, and not to be fenced and bounded by pure individuality, and one wondered sometimes if Clapham, or Balham, or Camberwell, those loved, unlovely places, were somehow helping these pilgrims from a far-off city.

My horse was done and could not be ridden. I left the head of the column and began to observe the men. First there was the sergeant-major, a great broad-shouldered fellow, seemingly as strong as an ox, yet, though he disguised his distress with an ironic smile, the signs of it were clearly upon him. Of course, it was impossible that he could ever "fall out," but the passing hint of it for a moment crossed my mind. Pardon, O giant of strength and endurance, that I indite these words, yet did not a like shadow flit sometimes across thy own cheerful vision? The first few sections of fours seemed to be going fairly well, till I came upon Twiggs, who was evidently hard put to it.

This boy, who passes through these pages unwounded, was fated to be killed in the Jordan Valley during a terrible raid. He stood out from all the other "men" of the company, peculiar in his physical and mental aspects. Small made and of almost perfect proportions, there was a dignity about his carriage that made me many a time speculate as to his descent. A touch of primness, and the fact that he had come out from England with us as officers' mess cook, gave him amongst the men the title *Mrs*. Twiggs, a joke that carried no scorn with it, for he was a competent and game youngster and a dead shot. How well I remember calling him into my hut on Salisbury Plain to show him the glories of our mess-kit, and how later in the support trenches in France the men would come round in the evening to the cook-house, to "call on Mrs. Twiggs."

He said he could "manage very well, thank you, sir," and was cheered by my statement that the company could not get on without him. Some distance behind him a really bad four was marching, and small wonder, for it included Egan, the light-weight, who boasted (it is the correct word) two conduct sheets, both covered with "crimes." This lad was convinced that because he had once been a flower-boy and had "come out of the streets," he was entreated hardly by everyone in the company, headed by myself, whom he was totally unable to understand. He always complained of his food, and for years past had from time to time indignantly held out for officers' inspection nasty-looking little pieces of bacon, or crusts of bread, asking riotously: "Is that a man's ration?" The answer generally was that it was quite sufficient for a child. He had a kind of weak alliance with a burlier person, also a malcontent.

Thunder by name, a heavy-weight, who had distinguished himself in the Balkans by abandoning rifle and bayonet during a raid, and laying out several Bulgars simply by hitting them under the chin. This man had once been my servant, but he hit a man on the nose on parade one day, conduct that could not possibly be overlooked, whatever secret amusement greeted it in the officers' mess. Shortly afterwards, after a period of pack-drill, he retired into private life. Neither of them loved discipline or understood it; both now were thoroughly "down."

With heads bent, both of them marching slightly behind the other two of the four, of whom one was a stalwart fellow who refused stripes at any price and wrote home for books on algebra, they did not respond for long to my treatment. They would buck up for a moment while you spoke to them and looked at them, but when you had passed their heads drooped and they would fall back into their old places, just slightly in the rear. An exasperating crew, but the end of their story is not yet

That five more minutes only remained before the rest would come was the thought uppermost in my fearful heart, as I watched the men. They simply would have to "stick it." The company had gone marching on in good repute through many a tough trek in Macedonia; it was not likely I was going to let it be done in by a wretched place with such a ridiculous name as Jemmameh. It could not be far off now; surely the worst was over.

And yet, as I thought of the energy that had been given out by these men, the long stretches of work accomplished and put behind us, I wondered if the breaking-point was at hand. Still pondering these things, I noticed that the head of the battalion had halted. At once I halted my own men and waved them the signal to fall out. Without a word they sank in their tracks. Their toiling energy left them like water from a broken vessel, as they collapsed *en bloc* at the shutting-off of effort. It was as if a machine-gun, suddenly turned on, had swept them all to death.

Like sixty watched seconds the magical ten minutes relentlessly passed, and once again at the summons the dog-tired men got up. At such a time there is need to be instant to watch and descend upon slackness or the slightest fault, else, by the slowness of one man, the whole company risks a fevered first five minutes of making up lost ground. We were just about to move off, and I was glancing down the column, when I noticed a man who apparently was making no effort to rise. Already the head of the battalion had started. Striding down the company, "What the devil's that man doing? Get up at once," I said.

Several voices broke out angrily from the men standing in the ranks about him. "He's out. He's fainted." The company began to move.

"Open out your ranks, then," I answered, "and let the stretcher-bearers do their job." What a brute I was. How I wished I had not fallen into that mistake!

We moved on. The fainted man was left behind in the dust. I guessed our field ambulance would follow us up some time that day, but dared not breathe a hint of it to the men. For, however steeled to their task, knowledge of possible assistance in the rear saps endurances that would stick it a little longer, did no alternative exist to present pains but certain and utter abandonment. To these men the battalion, the company, was everything in this far-off land, where all else that made life companionable was exploded. They would not have fallen out for anything, so dear to them this military society they had come to accept in lieu of parents, home, and business. They loved what of-tentimes they cursed. The spirit of the pack was strong.

Something could be descried in front of us, a squat mud build-ing, the rise of a small low bridge. This provided an interest that lured us through the intervening barrenness. Perhaps it was the place we sought. But no, it was too small, too isolated. The column now was moving very slowly: at last, we made the bridge. To the left a small well stood, but it did not raise one solitary hope, for the gear was broken and it hardly looked able to serve anyone with water.

Here were queer places for storing grain, cut into the ground like tanks and built over, with square holes in the centre. In the narrow black shadow, the bridge cast, a man of another company sprawled, pallid-faced, a ghastly spectacle.

I cursed him in my heart for falling out and making a sight of him-self, depressing to us, who laboured on. Past the village huddled forms displayed themselves, mere heaps of equipment, pitiful affairs. The last lap was taking its toll of us now. News came up to me: Judson, Bilboys,

Howard have fallen out. "O damn!" was all I could reply. But several men of the companies in front of mine, who had chucked it up, it appeared, a little too lightly, I ordered to their feet, and drafted sternly into my own command, and marched awhile beside them, and made them come on. Sad were the contests with my own weaklings; loath I was in each instance to confess my powers beaten by the fatigue of another that was too strong.

And now the country began, almost imperceptibly, to change. Hills lay before us, the birthplace, it appeared, of the *wadi* that in the forenoon, again and again, had impeded us. We had passed before we knew it from those hot, level lands, and were winding in single file along a broken, ascending track. The pace, which had been so slow, quickened considerably, and we all scuttled along as fast as we could, afraid of losing touch with the company in front. Now that it seemed certain that the end of the march was near, everyone came on vigorously; the monotony of those last fatiguing periods was broken.

Here there was a cooler air; here, too, were difficulties of a different kind to encounter: the getting of the mules along a narrow way; the keeping of the men closed up on the slippery and unequal stones. It was a village we were nearing, a village with inhabitants, a place of life and movement. The speed became so great that I lost sight entirely of the company in front, whose last mules vanished in a rearward cloud of dust. For now, the track had broadened and become a trodden way again, and here was the village. And there, slightly below us to the left, were the wells, large, stone-built, well based, dating from antiquity. And our own engineers were about them. And there was water.

We passed beyond them, turned to the left away from the mud buildings—a village in southern Palestine is a chance-built affair, a collection of mud dwellings that have never even dreamed of forming a street—and formed up in companies on a fairly level piece of dusty ground. The march had come to an end. Officers and men, equally exhausted, took off their equipment, and began to taste at last the blessedness of rest. There was no need to hurry; it would not be dark for an hour or two.

As water was at hand, we could now take a good pull at our water-bottles. In a quarter of an hour's time, we should begin to think of bivouac grounds, somewhere quite near in these new and not unpleasant hills. For my own part, I was absolutely done—couldn't do a stroke more. Making an effort, I took my saddlebags off the back of my mare, who looked the very picture of lassitude, stumbled half-blindly to a

25

place—anywhere—in the dust near her, lay down with my head on one of them, and prepared myself for dreams.

But the devil who jerks the strings about when nations go to war could not abide so tranquil and innocent a spectacle. It irritated him. Foreseeing, with the characteristic cleverness of disembodied spirits, that we should be arriving at Jemmameh about this time, tired out, with peace in our souls, he breathed into the ear of the commander of a Turkish corps that the opportunity had come for a reconnaissance in force towards a place called Araki el Menshize, not many miles to the northeast of the spot where we were resting.

This we learnt many months afterwards. At the time we knew nothing, but only felt the results. All we were conscious of was that we were hungry and tired, and that we had been wantonly and evilly disturbed.

The news came suddenly, almost before my eyes had closed, by the mouth of fat Tattersley, one of my own runners, elevated some months ago to a place on headquarters staff. "Sir, the commanding officer wants to see you at once, and he says you had better come on your horse, as it is to find an outpost line." This was delivered breathlessly and with a kind of smiling joy. "Tatts" loved messages and seemed to treat war as a terrific joke. I hope he will come again into this story: he certainly shall, if memory and happy moments serve. For the boy was always a picture of radiant good temper, and worth tons of bar gold to any fighting formation.

I believe it was the breadth of his grin that got him a military medal at the taking of Beersheba. For he directed me wrong in that dramatic fight, and I should certainly not have recommended him for it then. He pals up with other delightful folk, long of my acquaintance, the runner Scutt, and the runner Smith. But now Tattersley and his news suffices.

With a dull kind of resignation, I got up and put on my equipment. Another outpost line! In front of Beersheba, at Beersheba, beyond Beersheba, and up to and including Sheria I had practised, till I was sick of it, this military operation, which comes, I believe, in the text-books under the wide heading "Protection when at Rest." Rest! we never seemed to have been at rest since the opening trek from Tel El Fara, and certainly there would be no rest again tonight. So, I thought, as I handed my company over to my second-in-command, and wondered what was up, and what was to be done about the mare.

For the brute was so utterly used up that she could hardly put one leg in front of another. Her bones stuck through her skin; she looked like a piece of meat for the knacker. I had never understood her, though we had had so many adventures together, from the time I took her off my second colonel, in England, because she stumbled on roads, and shied at mechanically propelled vehicles. I had not the heart to ride her, so I set off, tugging her along with me, an incubus, for her limbs were stiff and languid, but I was obeying orders, and it was just possible she could be kicked, on emergency, into a last lolloping trot.

On the top of a hill not far from ours I met the C.O., two of the other company commanders already with him. He spoke quickly. It was obvious the matter was urgent. An outpost line had to be established at once, because a Turkish corps was reported to be moving in our direction.

"It's a bloody nuisance," said the C.O., "but it's got to be done," and he fell to describing positions he thought we might take up in the jumbled mass of *wadis*, hills, downlands, and rolling plains that lay before us. Anyone who has listened to a colonel trying to tell you where to go, with a difficult landscape in front of him, when time presses, or has himself cut up a sector into smaller pieces for his subalterns, knows the weakness of words and how few most of us have to our tongues. For everyone has a private closet of colours which don't match with his neighbours', and each man looks at landscape with his own peculiar eyes.

At length, after some unbelievable misconceptions, the company commanders understood which was to take the right, which the centre, and which the left, and rushed off forthwith (on a guarantee that their companies would be despatched after them) to make a breathless closer acquaintance with the ground.

Choosing an outpost position is more difficult and more tiring than going with a lady to choose a hat. For it is not the misspending of a few pounds that hangs upon your choice, but the lives of men. Nor does ground render your work easy, for in open country there are generally two positions to choose from, one boldly pushed out, and one moderately well back.

But on this occasion luck was with me, for I had not hunted about long (the mare had been taken over by an orderly) before I lighted on a series of old trenches, facing in the direction I required, and admirably sited. They petered out towards the left, and I had some trouble in deciding how to link up with the company commander on that flank; but presently he came along, and we settled it amicably. The commander of the company on my right decided to go some distance forward, and there was another company beyond him, lost in obscurity. No one was in reserve. The position to be held was both wide and complicated. We put all our irons in the fire.

I could never understand who dug those trenches, for from the Turks' point of view they faced in the wrong direction. They must have been dug for practice, a long time ago. It was evident that our cavalry had had a fight there some days previously, for the ground was littered with packs and equipment, and I found later a number of excellent bivouac poles, made in short sections to fit together, and some light hardwood pegs, all used by Turkish cavalry.

The company was upon me almost before I had done, and I sent them to their posts straightway and sited my headquarters. Everyone was "fed up" at this unexpected turn of affairs, but they took it as all in the day's work, being old hands and well broken in. I did not feel disposed to treat the rumoured Turkish corps very seriously, though I dared not gamble on the off-chance that nothing would happen. We held a very strong position, and later on I discovered that two machine-gun teams had drifted up without reporting, and had established themselves in two of the strongest places in the line. I had hardly arranged all this, got dixies of water for the men (after a great deal of trouble, for the wells were not yet properly repaired and the supply was short) when an absolutely black night came down upon the scene.

But before that happened, I gave one of my sergeants a piece of meat that had been served out as a special dainty to myself and the other company officers, at Sheria. Not knowing what to do with it, I had wrapped it in the only clean piece of stuff I could find—a yellow flag belonging to the Turkish railway. The meat was now very well-seasoned, but I thought that perhaps the sergeant would relish it. I gave it him that evening. I learnt afterwards that he buried it during the night. I often wish I had kept the flag it was wrapped in; with it went one of our few relics of the capture of Sheria.

3: "Fetching A Compass"

In the grand sense nothing happened at Jemmameh. The Turkish corps returned to its quiet pastures at Hebron, where it remained, under the severe eye of the Fifty-Third Division. Thereupon our outpost line, which we had chosen in such a hurry, became rather an absurd thing, and after we had handed it over to another unit of the brigade, fell into military disrespect. But several minor events, dear to men's hearts though not noted in despatches, made our sojourn linger in my memory. For reinforcements arrived. And it rained. And there was a cigarette issue. And I got a bath.

The cigarettes were brought up, together with some canteen stores, by the wicked major who had made that culpably cheery forecast of the tortuous march that brought us to Jemmameh. This officer, gifted with great but chaotic energy, was happiest when he had wheedled two limbers out of the colonel and departed on some frightfully adventurous campaign of his own into vast back areas, whence, after struggles with all sorts of wild people, he would reappear when he was quite forgotten, at the head of a little cavalcade.

My experiences are confined, unfortunately, to second-hand accounts of his doings in these remote places. He is credited with several stiff encounters with the Bedouins, who are wont to haggle overmuch concerning the price of fowls, and I know he has taken more than one canteen absolutely by storm.

The rain happened one night, and must not be taken too seriously or confused with the real thing. It was a light overture, played on muted strings, welcomed rapturously by the audience, and tantalizing because it left off too soon. A few big drops that fell through the darkness. How clearly, I can see the little bivouac under whose low-pitched sheets I was lying asleep when it came. Rain! At the first heavy patter I woke outright, crawled out, and held a large copper pot to a corner of the roof. There was a general stir throughout our small encampment: everyone was holding out receptacles. Cheerfully and excitedly, we called to each other. We were very glad.

The last rain had been a freak shower early in September at Sheikh Nuran, and did not count. That excepted, I had not seen any since I was in hospital at Salonica, the day when the division marched to the quay en route for Egypt, and the beds were drawn into the centre of the ward. Thus far our thirsting imaginations prowled for a sign of any. It ceased after about three minutes. Then we stretched ourselves for sleep again, annoyed at the parsimony of heaven. It paid us back right enough, later on.

As for the bath, it was such a personal and private act that I hesitate to recreate it. But this too is of importance, if what weighed then is to weigh now in this narrative. I cadged it off our field ambulance, whose officers seemed to be conducting the campaign amid the luxury of a drawing-room. This remark they will particularly resent. I found them, on the second day after our arrival, camped magnificently under the lee of a neighbouring hill. From the aspect of the officers' quarters, which contained several collapsible washstands and more than one folding chair, you might have supposed them leading a quiet depot life at Kantara, the canvas city on the Suez Canal.

Sneaking around in search of a square—or even triangular—meal, I noticed in front of a bivouac a bath, with water in it. The captain to whom it belonged was a fairly old acquaintance of mine—we had ridden alongside each other, camp-prospecting, in Macedonia. The rest is pure bliss. The quartermaster gave me a clean shirt: I returned to the company a remade man. Never can I possibly forget it, though years of quiet life in England roll between. It is one of those live points that glow for ever in memory.

Reinforcements is a big word, but the strengthening that came to us here was one of quality rather than quantity. For now, bearing with them many tales of wanderings and hard adventures, the men who, according to orders, had been left behind at the opening of the campaign, managed to overtake us, accompanied by several of the first wounded, now healed and happy and ready to fight again. The clan-ship of Londoners is wonderful. These men were extraordinarily glad to rejoin us, and we to welcome them, nor did any small matters of temporary official status relinquished to returning sergeants or corporals make jealousy mar the welcome.

Here I got again my lamp-post sergeant, Challard, a tremendous fellow with a small high-pitched voice, who advertised the battalion by taking fourteens in boots, which had to be specially constructed for him by the Ordnance. The last time I saw him he was sitting up in bed in hospital at Alexandria in a white night-shirt.

We moved from Jemmameh on the fifth, day of our stay, entirely ignorant of what was toward, or exactly where we were going. The battle of Sheria, coming after the fight at Kauwukah, and the capture of the defences at Beersheba had entirely satisfied for a time the lore of adventure in all of us—a love that in very many had never existed. Our "little Revenge" was quite ready to sink in the island crags or be lost evermore, or at any rate for a week or two, in some quiet bivouac ground amid the *wadis* of these rolling plains. In this mood, still greedy for rest and averse to further fame, we began a march that was a complete contrast to that of six days before.

The companies paraded near their bivouac grounds in separate columns, and wheeled off in turn after headquarters without the slightest fuss. Great care had been taken to leave the ground absolutely clean—a matter of routine, but not always successfully executed—and nobody had any complaints to make to anybody. The march was easy and not unpleasant, and for nine-tenths of the way without incident, but about one o'clock, or thirteen hours, we came upon a remarkable piece of country. It was a *wadi* that wind and rain had furrowed deep into the ground, a large, dry watercourse bounded on the left by high white cliffs, apparently of chalk, sheer and of grotesque shape.

Something of the same kind we had seen on the day we marched into Beersheba, while traversing the broken country on the way to that miserable town. Passing along this *wadi*-bed, and at last crossing it, we were surprised and delighted to see, not far in front of us, the green reeds of a stream, and note the slow passage of a little shallow water, a torrent at its last gasp, waiting for the rains.

Crossing it and looking over our right shoulders, we could see that, higher up, it had widened out into a kind of quagmire, in which some pioneers were standing up to their knees, trying apparently to rid it of certain dead bullocks, cast in by the Turks, in order to foul the water. In front bosomed a stubble-field, rather bare, but free from stones, a good camping ground. Without ceremony each company chose a bit of it and speedily erected its "bivvies."

An idea got about soon after our arrival that we were destined to stay for several days. Everyone therefore relaxed still further, and a certain atmosphere of content came into the camp, as we thought of the stream, and the bathing in puddles of water that perhaps awaited us on the morrow. An order had been circulated that on no account, either for drinking or washing, was it to be interfered with, a reasonable command, for everyone knew that the pioneers had the matter in hand. The field was hilly and very bare, not a scrap of wood, or even a loose large stone, anywhere; nothing but short, stiff stalks—of barley, I think.

On the left front of my own portion of the field it sloped into an off-shoot of a not precipitous *wadi*, and here, prospecting for wood immediately upon arrival, I found an empty ammunition box, just in advance of another officer, who noticed it a few seconds too late. The usual issuing of rations and careful distribution of water from the tanks carried by the camels—in my company we were accustomed to parade all water-bottles and fill them through tin funnels—closed an eventful day. Our life was becoming almost an idyll.

Heralded by none of the shy unfoldings that grace a Western dawn, earth presented us next morning with a naked sun, lidless, innocent of

CAMELS GOING THROUGH A WADI

clouds, a "broad and burning eye." We had grown accustomed to these blushless beginnings and woke early to the call of them, disturbing ourselves early in order to avoid the heat.

One of the first things I did on getting up was to clear a new site for my bivouac and get rid of all the stalks and prickles. Crawling up and down a small piece of ground, my servant and I accomplished after much trouble this finicking job, and together we re-pitched the sheets. On a very slight slope, so that the head of my valise rested a degree higher than the foot, it looked an inviting little domicile, with the striped woollen mat I had found at Beersheba spread out in front of it. These preparations were just completed when a message came:

"Prepare to move camp at once."

A scene of hurry followed in which everyone appeared to be exercising his authority over everyone else without any visible result. If you comment that we must have been very undisciplined, I answer that this is the chronicle of a toiling and striving multitude much vexed and harried, and that we were neither angels nor professional soldiers, or likely for a few æons to become either. It became at once evident that, though we had got up early, all the usual morning preparations were behindhand. The men could not be induced to adjust their movements to the changed situation, though repeatedly urged to "buck up" and "get a move on." The quartermaster-sergeant stood amidst a chaos of rations, meticulously issuing out fragments to chance-comers.

Men sat against a background of the gables of many bivouacs, quietly consuming their breakfast or absorbed in an extremely careful putting on of refractory *puttees*. I may have seen all this through the oblique vision of my own impatience, but certainly things seemed to be slack and out of hand. Nor did I make these observations until it was too late, for I was absorbed in getting the officers' portion of my encampment cleared up and ready to move, knowing by experience that our own mess-kit and our own valises had on more than one occasion been discovered unready when the time came.

I thought that by this time the company could be relied on to come up to the scratch without being hounded, and it was with very bitter feelings that I joined the column late, leaving behind me an unclean camping ground.

Another company had been caught out in the same way, and was wheeling into position as I arrived, but this was no balm for me when the colonel, a young regular soldier, rode up and let off some caustic remarks. On the march, at the first opportunity, I did the natural thing—bit off the head of my company-sergeant-major in private, letting him know, with some directness, that it was to him that I, the military leader, looked for right management of these domestic matters. He deserved some of it, but the blame clung unpleasantly to us all.

After we had all cooled down and this unfortunate business had sloped into the past, we began to take note of where we were going. Before long, it became evident—indeed, I had been informed by the adjutant—that we were about to loop the loop and return to Sheria. Great the indignation of these "Children of Israel" (as I was wont to call the men on account of their grumbles) when the purport of the march was understood. To think that they had perspired forward to Huj, and carted themselves wearily to Jemmameh, only to be packed incontinently back to the place whence they had set out.

A dim recognition that it was owing to a difficulty of feeding us, because we had lent our transport to another corps for some special purpose, did not do much to allay their indignation. They thought they were being trifled with, "messed about," in their own direct phraseology, and they hated themselves, their higher commanders, and above all Palestine, offering it freely, on derisive tongues, a gift to the world in general. This sarcastic violence was of course the outcome of a mood, but I truly believe that they prefer the green of Camberwell Green to any other colour, and the rectangularity of Buskin Park (about which we have composed a ballad) to the magnificently open spaces of Philistia.

Sheria was associated in our minds with a troubled night, a ragged hole-and-corner battle, and hordes of flies. We had been tormented by flies for weeks, but I think it was at Sheria that a large number of them decided to abandon the seductive society of dead bodies and follow the further adventures of the living. Organising themselves as only modern creatures can, they waited until we had fallen in and were ready to move off, when lo! each horde of buzz-mates selected a man and settled themselves securely upon his pack. Vainly we tried to disturb them: they simply rose, circled heavily about, and then sat down again. With a certain grim humour, we saw that we were doomed to act as porters to these tormentors. The packs were black with them: they would not go away.

But directly we arrived at any camping ground and began our domestic labours, they too had their affairs to see to, took part in the issuing of rations, tasted the sugar, and finally chose each his bivouac for the night. Now we were taking them back to their old haunts. It is difficult to render correctly the part played by the flies in these early days of the campaign: in a cavalry war, when many horses are slain, it is impossible to deny them food. Detestable creatures, they increase almost while you look at them. Those who have warred in Palestine can understand the presence in the Old Testament, as one of the more important devils, of Beelzebub, The Lord of Flies. Did they offer him bluebottles in his temple, and sing hymns to him in low, buzzing chorus? But I grow irreverent

The distance to Sheria from the bivouac ground we left so suddenly was about ten miles, and by this time we had covered three-quarters of that distance. We marched with the railway, which ran, on a slight embankment, to our left, and just before the midday halt passed a fine large culvert of solid masonry, which the Turks, who had built it quite recently, probably with German assistance, had not been able to destroy. I thanked them ironically in my heart for presenting us with such an excellent piece of work. Along this railway we could see the figure of an officer proceeding slowly and deliberately, in field-boots, taking his own time, and seemingly not responsible to anyone.

Looking at it carefully, I recognised Bloomes, the most eccentric and indispensable officer in the brigade. Almost every brigade has an officer vaguely related to him, but there is only one Bloomes in the world: I am sure he will pardon me saying that he stands alone. Chartered by common consent to draw a cheque for any amount on the world's social bank, Bloomes could not be said to belong to any city or continent, though I think business ties had connected him in the past somehow with South America. But both words are inappropriate, for business in the fussy self-important sense was absolutely unknown to him, and he never had any ties.

Not young and yet not old, but decidedly game, he occupied a midway position in the stream of time, politely refusing to be carried along by it. In the most "fly" and knowing circle you can imagine sitting in a private room around its drinks, Bloomes, adding himself quietly to the selected, would soon be deferred to as more "fly," more sociable, and more knowing. He bestowed on all the benediction of his smile, suiting it always with a word or a phrase from his own peculiar mint. Generals coming on tours of inspection he dealt with firmly, quietly and graciously, remarking on the beauty of the landscape, the inclemency of the weather, and the curiously long duration of the war.

Nobody has ever taken a rise out of him, or has wanted to; and against a quarrel I have always understood he has a carefully oiled pistol.

Of all the officers I have met, he is the one I should choose to have with me in a tight place. He went after strange jobs. You would never find his name in the official scratchings. Some misty business connected with the administration of canteens, added to the post of warden of the brigadier's bag and keeper of his travelling-carpet, had for many months severed him from his battalion duties. Bloomes was a teller of stories, not always suitable for the printed book. Bloomes was an arranger of entertainments. Bloomes was, in short, in the best sense of the word, a cove.

He came up to us at the halt, and we conversed upon that fascinating subject, the ways and means of obtaining bottled beer. With large promises he left us, resuming his solitary trek. And now we drew near to the very battlefield where we had risked all nearly ten days before. Great was the interest displayed by the men as they came to recognise each separate feature. The white building, we had lately passed was the place where the Turkish battalions emerged for their counterattack. Now we were on the very positions the defenders held. Little heaps of head-cover still remained on the light ground, showing the successive lines held by the sections as they retired.

Here where the railway curved to the left through a cutting was the position we had lately held, and here the yeomanry, in a knee-to-knee charge, had burst through and cleared the country. Places where desperate deeds are done have a sanctity about them: to re-encamp in that neighbourhood was to bivouac between the lines of history. For in open warfare there is no jumble or confusion of the issue. "Here," we could say, "we decided that affair, and the battle moved over against Huj."

We arrived at our camping ground early in the afternoon, after passing an enormous enemy ammunition dump which, as they had distributed it in little heaps over several acres, the Turks had not been able to destroy. We did not enter Sheria, but sat down on the barren desert outside—the most shamelessly bare place I have ever rested in. Here the colonel and his staff fell into a great fit of manual energy and delved a large hole in the ground, leaving a dirt table in the centre and dirt seats. This they did to distract themselves from thoughts of their kit, which together with that of all the other officers had been stowed in baggage wagons that had gone off in the wrong direction. The colonel's impromptu mess was on an old battery position still marked by a heap of shell cases, the only objects visible on the plain.

Just before dusk we lifted up our eyes and beheld the wagons, labouring heavily along, the transport men who drove them grumblingly inquiring for the positions of the various battalions. Horses and men were alike dead tired, and we, who had so often undergone similar experiences, long, obscure, not easily vehicled in words, had plenty of sympathy for them, and readily pardoned their hurt ironic sentences. And now a scouring party licensed by me in the late afternoon to go in search of wood returned, loaded with bits of quartering and match-boarding, reporting unimagined plunder of that kind not very far off, in a neighbouring hollow.

There was, too, a Bedouin encampment, said a company commander, coming over to ask where in the name of wonder we had pinched the wood from; it lay, he said, in a fold of the ground north-easterly, not very far from our camp. Next morning, he went there on a fowl-purchasing expedition, and was received in great state by the head man, who invited him into a large bivouac and offered him food. The purchasing of the fowl, a heated discussion conducted entirely by signs, was not an easy matter.

When the tongues of his wives and ministers rose too high for the forbearance of savage or civilized man, the chief would turn and roar orders at them and they would sit silent or slink out of the tent. A fine old despot, and much admired by the officer who has sole rights of reproduction of an inter-scene I can only hint at. As, towards lunch-time, there was a litter of feathers in his lines, I believe the purchase or acquisition was finally successful.

Next morning, intently watched by the Bedouins, who were longing to pounce on the wood we were leaving, perforce, behind us, we bade farewell for the second time to Sheria. It was not necessary to do more than collect the material roughly into heaps, for we knew that as soon as we had turned our backs it would be dragged away by dozens of long-gowned children. The chief gift I left for these nomads was a painted and grained yellow wooden washstand, with which my men had presented me, a great prize, on the preceding day.

It was one of those awful contrivances that have a circular hole cut for a china basin, and I could not, of course, make the slightest use of it. I doubt whether a piece of suburbia has ever been so entirely detached from its natural surroundings.

We were now on our way to Hareira, *en route* for Gaza, and great was the speculation as to the meaning of this new move. It would bring us to the coastal sector, to the sea, miles away from any enemy, for by this time General Bulfin's corps was over thirty miles north of the town, fighting, or about to fight, for the possession of what was later known as Junction Station, a place where the Beersheba and Jerusalem railways joined. Could it be that we were being taken to the coast to bathe and refit, and make ourselves strong and lusty for the campaign's next stage? Already we had looped the loop, and now were going leftwards. The seaside idea held the imagination of most, but the issue of serge tunics at Hareira, which we reached after a short march, made the breezes of rumour blow all ways at once.

Here, where some gentle rain fell, a warning that the impending deluge could not now long be delayed, we meditated waterless on our fate, while Coborne, our plump, popular and well-liking Lewis-gun officer, was saddled with the thankless task (generally performed by the major) of going back to Sheria with the water-camels, under instructions to catch us up when, where, and how he could. There was a meat issue at Hareira, the sort of thing that goes down pat in everybody's diaries, but for me this indeterminable one-night's lodgement is chiefly remarkable for having possessed a tree.

The next day we set out for Gaza itself, a place that for many months I had wished to see. We followed a track that led us round and about downlands, with little deep, gulf-like *wadis* cracking them open here and there occasionally. This land had a slight shimmer of green about it; we were coming, we thought, to better pastures, the air was cooler, everyone felt glad. About midday there was a long halt, near a scoop in the ground where cracked mud showed the remains of a saltish pool. I took advantage of this halt to stew rapidly in a shell-hole the meat I had saved from the previous day, when our hospitable field ambulance folk had given me a feast.

A tough and unsatisfying repast, though I could not avow it, for at Sheria I had thrown a bombshell into our mess by declaring suddenly that henceforth everyone was to cook for himself. There had been domestic bickerings in the past which I was no longer prepared to brook. This was the beginning of the new regime: I had to pretend I was getting on very well and liked it.

It was a long march, but full of interest, for from time to time we kept coming upon signs of the recent fighting. Turkish forward gun positions, as we drew nearer, were passed on our left, with well-trenched covered quarters for the men. Then we noticed on our right a couple of dummy guns, made of wood, with shell-holes all about them. Shell-holes, too, of a large size fretted the sand; it was almost like one of the few quiet sectors in France. Gaza means much to some of our sorely-tried divisions, but I have not at my fingers' ends the military geography of its neighbourhood, and can only tell what we, innocent of it all, saw that pleasant afternoon. As we drew nearer stretches of sand appeared, the real coarse sand of the desert.

Over the last skyline the town itself came into view, but not clearly, for it is screened on the south by many plantations and cactus hedges. In front the track fell slightly towards an expanse of low ground which spread Gazawards, ending, not far from the cactus hedges, in a great hill of sand, cobwebbed with wire and furrowed with smashed and collapsing trenches, one of the Turks' last main positions. There had been wild flowers by the way as we traversed the last miles of our journey, and now still greener grass and deep red poppies greeted our eyes. The low ground that lay before us was a sweep of green, and there was room enough on it to have camped a division.

"A bad place for a bivouac," I said to my sergeant-major, as we approached; "I hope we shall not stop here: it looks fine enough now, but we should be properly caught on that marshy place if it rained."

This started a discussion in which the idea of a sudden downfall was scouted. As usual, there was not a cloud in the heavens. It looked as if the weather would never break. The dark cactus compounds, the white sandhills by the sea, the bluish-green grass with the red poppies growing in it, and beyond the sandhills the blue Mediterranean made the pleasantest of composed pictures. And now we were marching on the plain itself, and other troops were appearing. Evidently the division was concentrating, and we, too, were to bivouac on the marshes.

CHAPTER 2

Gaza and Beyond

1: A NIGHT AT GAZA

"Anyone coming to explore Gaza?"

Trobus wouldn't; he and his servant were absorbed in cooking arrangements—something that would show us how it really could be done. Jackson couldn't; somebody had to be on duty, and it was his turn. None of the officers of any of the other companies were willing to start out on a private expedition after a long march. I was about to set off alone, when Temple, my third subaltern, strolled up and said, in his mature, languid voice, "I'll come, skipper, if you like." I was delighted. We agreed that there was no time to lose, and set out at once together.

Temple, who carries his pack through this story, only to meet his death, poor boy, on the heights above Jerusalem, had been in my company longer than either of the other remaining subalterns. All my officers have been remarkable men; this one, younger in many respects and at the same time infinitely older than the others, was my solitary pure intellectual. Impatient of restraint, loathing many of the things I loved and specialised in—manual labour, for example—he was by no means at bottom the bit of a mug I at first took him for.

There is nothing so sad—I write this with a sense of abject penitence—as false judgments made on men by those in authority over them, and I have made plenty. Yet considering our dissimilarities we got on very well together, take it all round, and I would not have lost him, nor he gone to another company, for worlds. Before the campaign, before the grand opening chorus of the guns at Beersheba, our friendship had mainly grown up on a literary basis: we both loved and consumed many books. But in these latter days, and especially after

Sheria, that basis had been broadened and reinforced by the spectacle of his behaviour. Temple, in fact, the other Temple, was rapidly growing up before my eyes, breaking rapidly down the ridiculous barriers of mere years that get too much attention paid their clumsy selves in the maze of human life.

We left the bivouac ground, now covered with acres of little brown gables set squatly on the herbage and crowded where it stretched towards the road with the more complicated scene made by the supply services and divisional technical appendages: dumps of beef and biscuits; ricks of compressed fodder suddenly come into being; the signal section with its more pretentious tents built round their own parti-coloured poles; lorries, wagons with men picking hasty meals beside them; an operating tent, used now by the ambulance unit as an officers' mess: all the picturesque flotsam and jetsam that feed, tend, and bring news to the great divisional show when camels, tractors, horses, donkeys, and lorries move it on the road to war.

On this we were careful to look back time and again, noting our path, for darkness might possibly be falling ere our return, and I did not wish to lose my way belated. We proposed first to explore the Turks' strong-point—it was, I believe, the famous place called Ali Muntar— get right on to the top of it, and, our bearings taken, make a bee-line for the city. The place struck us as being enormously strong—a glacis, defended by belt upon belt of wire, much of it still intact.

But once through this protection the fortified hill showed what a tremendous bombardment it had sustained. The soil was light, and merged in many places into sand. The deep passages that had been cut in every direction over it had everywhere collapsed, though it was not easy to see how much of the ruin was due to the impossibility of keeping trenches intact at such angles in such a substance and how much to the effects of gun fire.

Plunging heavily about this forsaken confusion, we finally struck the road on the left of the hill, a track choked with deep loose sand, bordered on the left by tall ten-foot-high broken hedges of prickly-pear. The road was full of horses led by men, who all asked us where the watering place was. but we could not tell them, and after trudging slowly and laboriously along for about a hundred yards on the very edge of it, we took advantage of a long opening and cut across a piece of once cultivated ground. Immediately we found ourselves in the first of a series of plantations, small sparse orchards of fig-trees all hedged round by cactus or prickly-pear.

Dodging through holes in these hedges, we hurried quickly on, passed a wrecked waterwheel, the familiar "*saqqia*" of Egypt, and many shells and shell-boxes, evidence that the Turk had made good use of this cover for his guns. At length we broke into a fringe of houses, and found that we had entered the city at its lower and poorer quarter, the southern lee of the slight rise on which the principal buildings stand.

The streets were very quiet, the place almost entirely deserted. Forsaken by the original inhabitants, who had long ago passed away into the heart of Palestine, only a stray wandering native or two haunted in a shifty way these abandoned homes. The dwellings in this part of the town were of mud, though the *mosques* were of stone. The streets were mere passages that interminably crossed and intersected, so narrow and shut in that a careless wanderer would speedily get lost. We entered a *mosque*, a place with an open courtyard of stone, several small stone chambers or cells, and a well. Nearby a minaret of fretted stone, delicately carved, lifted its ancient shaft to the sky. Nine-tenths of the way up a gallery of dark latticed wood had been built round it, which marred the excellence of its symmetry: but I bore it away with me in my mind as the most beautiful structure in Gaza.

There were some camels in one of the narrow streets, being loaded by natives of the "*Gippy*" Labour Corps with stones for the continuation of the new railway which had lately been pushed at top speed from the country south of the city. On our progress towards the city itself we suddenly came across the track, the great strong permanent way, driven clean through the streets amongst the debris, with acetylene flares placed at intervals, and telegraph poles running alongside. It was the strangest contrast, this ruthless military invasion of the old by the new, for Gaza was as ancient as the city of a fairy-tale, shaken to pieces by enchantment while yet it lay asleep.

Here was a desolation that rivalled anything in France, for though we searched diligently no furniture or fittings remained in the length and breadth of it except one small piece of guttering, the end of a bedstead, and a pile of smashed woodwork in a garden, which had apparently been overlooked.

Picturing this wilderness of stone houses as a populous city, filled with men and women habited in all the gay and sad colours of the East, we walked in silence up the main thoroughfare, a slow ascent which brought you at the crest to a public place for drawing water, a fine array of ancient stonework, as unlike the ordinary English drinking-fountain as a suburban "Elizabethan" house is to the lordly dwellings of old to which it claims affinity. Here an archway led into a large stone-paved courtyard or market-place, with a fountain and circular basin in the centre. Large numbers of shells lay about it, which led us to suppose that women had pitches here for the selling of shell-fish, like our own flower-girls where Love shoots his arrow in Piccadilly Circus. What a chattering and hubbub rose here not so very long ago and down the ages! Now it was all dry and quiet, the water conduits broken, everyone departed.

We rambled for an hour, visited the great *mosque*, in which it has been said the Turks stored ammunition, lost our way, peeped into the stone chambers of houses, and wandered north-westward towards the sea, where large public-buildings of a modern cast stood grandly back from a broad road with paving-stones, a *trottoir*, and a kerb. A large cemetery cumbered with big stone tombs looking very desolate ended with everything else in heaps of shifting sand-dunes and the sea. This street was torn and cratered by the passage and landing of enormous shells, good proof that the navy had "effectually co-operated" with the forces on land.

Walking down this road and turning at length to the right, we next re-entered the city from the north, and found ourselves at once in the potters' quarter, a series of terraces heaped with the debris of centuries, over which all kinds of odd-shaped houses had crept, and into whose lower slopes the potters had driven their rough low factories. To regain the town's more regular alleyways took some time, as the terraces were divided from each other by loose stone walls only at odd places climbable. But at length we got into a small evil street and began to make for "home," the chilly little bivouac shelters in the marshes, now a long way off. We were near the highest portion of the city and had recognised a street we had been in before, when, slowly and deliberately, down came the rain.

The afternoon was now far advanced and a common greyness hid the sky. At first, hoping a little hopelessly that it would stop, like the sudden midnight shower at Jemmameh, we crept into the first shelter that stood handy, a large vaulted chamber of stone, evidently where something had been manufactured. But the rain grew heavier and the hour was late: we decided to make a bee-line for the distant camp. Hurrying down a street that seemed to have been the town's main shopping centre, we came to a square and a garden, where three soldiers were living, all by themselves, in a bell tent.

These were the only persons we saw in Gaza, a few old folk in the lower and poorer part excepted. A little further on we came upon a pile of old sandbags, carefully stacked and emptied. Several of these we tied together, making two rough coats, a fair protection for a short time against the weather.

It was not long before we had left the last building behind us and were plodding heavily through the fig-tree plantations. Both of us now were very tired, and quiet, and rather dejected. The wrecked city had made us sad. We felt lonely and homeless and belated. And towards what were we struggling over the sodden, slippery ground?— a low marsh, soaked with rain, and two thin draughty sheets with an opened-out valise inside them. A miserable business. There was nothing, as children say, "to look forward to." Yet wherever the battalion camped was home to us, and we feverishly stumbled on to get there as soon as possible. Temple was clinging on to an ammunition box he had picked up and hoped to cut some dry splinters out of for a fire to boil cocoa on; I held fast to a large empty biscuit-tin. Darkness fell as we found our way through the last cactus hedge and crossed the road to the old strong-point. Here, after much forlorn wandering in a maze of sandy pits, we got to the top, and looked down upon the marsh.

The scene was both picturesque and bewildering. The camp, which seemed to have spread far and wide in every direction during our absence, was now indicated to us in the general blackness by hundreds of little lights masked partially under stretched wet sheets. Everyone who could afford the luxury had lit his carefully husbanded candle. All the distinctive marks we had noted so carefully on our outsetting were gone. Battalion mingled with battalion in that confusion of dim illumination. Here and there, and especially near us, at the edge of the road that ran round the base of the hill, a blazing bonfire marked the headquarters of a lucky unit or the whereabouts of the supply services, never at a loss for firewood.

Looking down upon this gipsy-like scene, we could not help meditating on the immense number of men wrested from their occupations to follow with one accord the common calling of war and supported with all the necessities of life day after day in these wildernesses. If all this could be done now, what mightier miracles of unity and social effort Peace could accomplish, if only we rightly could invoke her aid. Such a train of thought would have led, in our old mess at Sheikh Nuran, where we were all alone together, to violent discussion, broken by the excited "No, but look here!" of one who, alas! would never more join in.

But Temple, generally an eager protagonist, had nothing to answer now, and it was in silence that two tired adventurous men helped each other painstakingly and deliberately through the remains of the Turkish wire, and after many inquiries and fruitless journeyings in wrong directions, returned to their own particular portions of the general wetness.

If men are capable of greater happiness than the beasts that perish, they are also liable to sink deeper into the pits of wretchedness. An animal has its fur; a soldier, with only scanty manufactured stuffs to protect his sensitive skin, with the very hairs on his head often cropped close to his scalp, has worse nights in the world at times than bedless street cats or wandering tawny lions. Considerations among which his personal comforts are not numbered, hard facts relating to the transport of food-stuffs and accessibility of water, pin him down to places not of his choosing and where of choice he would never be. He cannot, like the animals, wander at will to look for a decent lair, but must lie down with only his mate's body to warm him when and where his officer directs, on marsh, or plain, or barren stony upland. He depends on cooked food, the greatest of all nuisances, and spends endless time and trouble over the preparing of miserable portions of it.

Surely man was not sent into the world to have a good time or even so bend it to his will as to make a good time universally possible. There is something in him that demands difficulties, and enables him to triumph over them. But the way has black portions that let men know misery, and even the sunlit stretches alternate with deepest shadow. That is in the nature of things unalterable in the most Utopian of human kingdoms.

The masses have always been acquainted with these realities, amendable certainly, but essential to man's development on earth. The war has introduced them to many thousands who shuddered at their imagining and affected to ignore their meaning. I threw down my tin upon arrival and turned to grapple with events. It was still raining heavily, and the marsh, though not under water, was very wet.

On my way through our camp, I passed the place where, early in the afternoon, I had seen our energetic headquarters staff busy digging a mess. It was now a muddy hole, filling with water, with a muddied pick and shovel lying beside it. They had all crept into their little wigwams, each with its roof as tight as a drum, and each with its diminutive trench and drain.

Further on, looking for my own shelter, I tripped in the darkness over a cord that reached out from the corner of one long combined gable, the result of co-operative enterprise, and was met by a loud shout from the disturbed inhabitants—"Who the hell's that?" "Get out of it, you silly lunatic"—and recognised the sweet phraseology of my own men. "Sorry," I said; "it's O.C. company." Laughter within and, "Beg pardon, sir, we didn't know it was you." These persons evidently were not altogether unhappy. They were bedded down, and shared between them the luxury of a candle.

My own bivouac was dark and unsatisfactory-looking, and I wondered what my servant had been at since I had been away. I called him, and he came out, the picture of woe. A man of middle age, I had taken him on at Jemmameh after the sudden sickness and disappearance of a fair-weather youth who had turned out to be unequal to the trials of a campaign of movement. Picked out by the sergeant-major from my flock as a man of some experience (for he had come to us after a pretty long spell in France), Beattie had proved himself, even in the few days I had had him, a person of great goodness of character, void of selfishness, humble, willing and painstaking.

But he was getting on in years for a modern soldier, was not skilful with his hands or up to any natural shifts or dodges, lacked initiative, and was sometimes very slow. It seems ungrateful to criticize a devoted servant who has done you splendid service, but I am taking men as they come and dealing with them truthfully, perhaps sometimes with a kindly bias.

My tent, a very important adjunct to the story, consisted of four bivouac sheets buttoned together into one square and then hoisted up on three sticks, one for each end and one in the centre, and pegged down tightly to the ground along the sides. This left the ends open, but one I usually managed to close in a flimsy sort of manner by stretching across its triangularity an old ripped-up sandbag.

I had tried pitching these sheets in every possible way, and had fallen back at last on the stereotyped method. But my sticks were nearly a foot higher than the official ones, and this gave a touch of lordliness to the abode. By an act of arbitrary power, I had willed myself two more sheets than my neighbours by virtue of its being company headquarters, and I carried also a spare sheet for my servant, so that he could be self-contained and live near me.

There was nothing lordly about it at the present moment. How we were going to get a fire started I could not imagine. A little pile of sticks lay on the corner of a ground-sheet near the centre pole. Beattie had carried them from the last place and had luckily been able to keep them dry. But he had forgotten to trench the tent, and the wet was stealthily advancing inwards from the sides. I crawled inside, handed him out my trench-coat and set him to work.

Before he had finished, I had decided to let the man join his two sheets on to the end of mine and share the shelter. He was damp and tired and miserable, and so was I. We were, so to speak, both on a raft together. It was not much to offer; indeed, it was the only sensible solution for both of us. So together we made the rearrangement and fell to buttoning the wet unwilling sheets. The last upright was formed, wickedly enough, by his rifle. But neither of us cared for anything but the prospect of hot food. It was arranged that he should light a fire just under his end of the shelter, boil some soup, and cook some rice. I said I would provide two tin mugs of hot cocoa. How was it to be done?

That ingenious device for raising the temperature of food known by the childish title "Tommy's Cooker" had given hot meals to many a man in the first two or three days of the campaign. But the last had long since burnt out, and I had not by this date made the acquaintance of a lady in Alexandria who, taking a tip from the Italian Army, supplied her soldier acquaintances with hard little cylinders of newspaper boiled in paraffin wax, which, when a tongue has been cut out of them with a knife, burn for a long time and also give light. I had always thought there were sufficient calories of heat given out by a candle to cook food and keep a dinner hot afterwards, if only one could store them up.

The idea, possibly as old as the hills, had come to me on my way back from Gaza, when I saw the big biscuit-tin. I now enlarged the mouth of it, placed it on its side in the bivouac, and stuck a candle within, raised on some pieces of brick, so that the flame was very near the top of the tin. Exactly above the flame I placed a mug of water, and in less than a quarter of an hour' the cocoa was made. Later I tried two candles, but the heat within the tin melted both. It is important that the mouth of the tin is enlarged sufficiently to give the candle enough air, but it must not be cut near the top, or the heat will escape. Even if you have a fire, two or three of these tins placed together make excellent "hot-plates."

By this invention I claim a spiritual relationship to the Swiss Family Robinson, though I believe that pious family was German. I have never yet met a Swiss who answers to the name of Robinson. Hans and Fritz were industrious and ingenious youngsters, but I always secretly despised them for doing such an inordinate amount of praying.

After filling the tent with clouds of smoke, Beattie managed to produce the soup and rice, and we squatted together, enjoying a meal that has somehow lodged in my memory against all others. There was bully-beef too, and biscuits, a royal repast. Warmed and lifted up by food, we spoke together, but our talk was not of capital and labour or the tyranny of wealth, but rather of tent-pegs, whose diminishing numbers we discussed as earnestly as if they had been citizens of the Empire.

"You must not hit them so hard, Beattie," I said; "you break their heads."

"I try not to, sir, but those little Turkish ones are very hard and brittle."

"They pack very neatly. Do you know where out mallet is?"

"I have it here, sir. Mr. Trobus borrowed it this afternoon, but I got it back."

"Be very careful not to lose it. I pinched it in Macedonia. It is very likely to get stolen. How many pegs have we got?"

"Ten, sir—eight and two spare ones. I found one lying about this afternoon."

"You mustn't pinch from the company, Beattie. It's not done."

"No, sir; but I thought as how this one would come in very convenient."

To this there was no answer, and now the noise of someone feeling for the tent's opening announced the approach of orders. We were to move next morning north of Gaza, and, thank Heaven, at a reasonable hour. The runner was enveloped in a ground-sheet. I asked him to take the message on to the sergeant-major.

The candle was guttering on a brick. I gave Beattie a blanket, and he crawled off to his end of the tent. The rain still pelted down, but our small drain was doing its work. In two minutes, master and man were asleep.

2: THE RAINS

This may be regarded as an inter-chapter, dealing with the subject of rain. For though one could give a true enough account of the two days that followed our departure from Gaza by saying that *réveillé* was at a certain hour, and that we arrived at Esdud at about dusk and that a post came up when we were in a barley field, all these excellent and uninteresting facts, doubtless chronicled in a thousand diaries, are drenched and swamped and sponged out of existence in my mind by

48

the simple remembrance of rain that fell. I could not, without much questioning of fellow-soldiers, tell you the exact order in which things happened during that troubled time.

A dark cloud hangs over these events and a mist obscures them. My mind has confused the places at which we halted on the two nights, for both were dismal, and both barley fields. Was it at the first or the second that a bonfire was burning and a draggled native runner sold us our first oranges? Or did the oranges relieve the gloom of the first and the bonfire stir envy in us on the second? Those of my audience who were there will take pleasure in recasting the smelted fragments of this honest prose. It will have to stand as it is; I cannot alter it.

The morning was fine but cloudy when we packed up and squelched out of the marsh. Just before we left, Coborne, the unfortunate Lewis-gun officer and general undertaker of all those odd jobs that generally fall to a reliable junior, arrived with the water-camels, a miserable string of prehistoric beasts of surpassing ugliness, led by equally miserable natives, shivering with cold, clothed in thin cotton gowns, and often with dirty bandages hiding cuts on their bare feet. Coborne had had one of those obscure experiences that represent so much to the individual and never get into print or even obtain for a few moments a sympathetic hearing among friends.

It is probably because the heroes tell them so badly, marring that curious tales as they elaborately set them forth with the cumbrous aid of spoons and knives and forks in the secure but mournful fastnesses of base depots. In brief, he had had to return to Sheria, and had been overtaken by rain, and the camels had fallen down in the mud, but he had managed to bring them along—hoping no doubt to find us firmly established by the sea in some quiet refitting base. And here we were, just about to move. He got no pity and scant thanks. His mission was an affair of the past. He had done his job. Here were the camels. And now we had to get on.

Before we moved the colonel addressed us. A young regular, keen and nervous, he did not believe in honeyed words, but spoke straight and to the point, unlike the officer he succeeded, who had been an amazing rhetorician. Colonel Goddam's speeches always reminded me of one of Napoleon's, "Soldiers of Italy, you have disgraced yourselves," or a few curt words to that effect. During his introductory speech, just on the eve of the campaign, for he had only lately come to command us, he had apostrophised us as "a lot of bloody monkeys." Perhaps it was a true diagnosis. We remembered these things with no malice and some amusement. I have known him swerve into suavity in private, but seldom before the troops.

All by this time knew him to be young, brave, competent, cheerful, and devoted to duty. He had a trick of swishing about with a light stick, like the colonel of a friendly unit under whom he had served for a time in Macedonia. Both were young, energetic, anxious to get on, ready and eager to attack, prone to appear suddenly in the firing-line when their subordinate chiefs supposed them safely at headquarters. They are types of the younger commanders. They are good now: in ten years' time they will be even better.

I remember no more of his speech than that we were in for a long march and that we should be in competition with another brigade, and were to do something more than our best. I don't think he alluded to what by this time was beginning to be generally talked about—I mean the object of our journey. Nobody knew for certain, but there was a growing rumour that our division had been selected to take Jerusalem, and that we were now on the way. This had already begun to invest our movements with a romantic glamour which the coming two days were temporarily to extinguish. But it broke out again later on, and after-events raised it to a flame.

By midday, when we halted for our meal amid some tufts of rank grass, we had marched for about six miles. We had worked, at our first outsetting, well to the east of Gaza, and none of the battalion had entered it save Temple and myself. For a mile or so sand dunes rose on the left of us, for we had been very near the sea, and it was not long before we crossed the railway. Then the country became open, resembling that from Sheria to Huj, but with rather more signs of herbage. It could almost be called flat, but was in reality a series of gentle undulations. So far, the march had been monotonous but the going fairly good, for the extremely light soil had soaked up with avidity yesterday's heavy rain. The sky had been for some time overcast, but the long succession of hot fine days in Egypt and lower Palestine during the past months had built up a belief in most of us that this part of the world could not produce a deluge.

We had forgotten certain vivid sentences in the Old and the New Testament, or, if we remembered them, had come to regard them, with the incredulous air of a modern, as stories flavoured strongly by man's imagination, and forgot that literature feeds on reality and is a great deal nearer significant truth than some imagine. "*The rains descended and the floods came*" calls up a state of weather that I now know only too well, and well can I realise the plight of a man in such a season who had put up any kind of heavy stone building on the soil we were now treading.

As we finished our meal the air grew colder and a thin drizzle made us think of coats. The meal came hurriedly to an end and the men started walking about to keep warm. The serge tunics that had been served out two days back were very thin, and everyone was still wearing drill shorts. The officers had left their surplus kit many miles behind, and were travelling on thirty-four pounds, weight strictly enforced. Most of them still had the drill tunics they kept for the cold evenings in the days, not so long ago, though it seemed in another world, when we went to battle in our shirt-sleeves. And now the order came to reload mules, the column reformed, and we streamed away.

A figure of speech appropriate for the hours to come. The heavens this time were slowly and continuously preparing for something they had not treated us to since well-remembered Macedonian days. A sudden downpour is often a mere flash-in-the-pan, a thunder and lightning affair; dread rather, if you carry a pack in a column, the drizzle that intensifies and thickens when skies become a uniform colour and all cheerful hues die out of mind and landscape.

The chill rain that begins at shut of eve, pictured by Keats, was the rain that now, stolidly and helplessly put up with by the tramping files, soaked these plains which had waited the event so long. After the first hour the hopes of the sanguine ones who had been talking of a fine evening quietly collapsed, and about this time, too, the camels, who had been pressing the ground deliberately beside us on our left flank, began to slip, move slower, and fall to the rear.

The added weight of water on the clothing and equipment of the men began, in the second hour lapsed, to tell upon their spirits, which up to this had risen paradoxically to the zenith. We had been following a track which was in fact only a trodden portion of the plain; and now it had turned to that primitive mud loved of all nasty undeveloped creatures and hated by man. This was the plain across which, a month hence, the transport of an army slithered, slipped, struggled, collapsed, and laboured on again in desperate and just successful attempts to supply enough food to the fighting troops. We only knew, as we plodded across it, that however long or short the march might be, there were certainly no billets at the other end.

Towards Jemmameh we had sweated and cursed in the dust and heat, but we had known that at the end good dry ground awaited

TEN MINUTES HALT

us—no one had pictured anything else; now we knew, though no one mentioned the thought, that the stopping place, whatever it might be, had nothing but waterlogged ground for us. The unknown, always supposed to be terrible, has also sometimes its bright possibilities, but Macedonia is a thorough school in these matters, and the large majority of the men knew exactly what to expect. There is a hill called Saragol that our brigade at least will never forget. Up to today it had stood (bracketed with our arrival at a place called Mahmudli) as "the utter edge."

It is this certain absence of billets, however ruined or humble, that depresses the town-bred man who treks in a far country. Streets, shops, lamp-posts; a villa, a tram, a policeman and the cinema round the corner, these are his world, his excellent sufficiency. He does not wish to see the Seven Wonders, the ruined statue of Memnon, the remains of ancient Thebes. He will go to the Pyramids if he can take a tram to them. It is curious to reflect that he is now tramping in the rain towards Jerusalem because he happens to have inherited an Empire. But that is a place his mother told him about, and it has raised his curiosity.

We had now done about twelve miles and the time was half-past six in the evening. No one had fallen out, but the pace had become slower and slower, until the men hardly seemed to move. The camels had long since disappeared. No one took any interest in the landscape, a sodden, featureless plain. There were no sounds but the sploshing of boots in mud and the irritating clank here and there of a man's badly swung mess-tin. No one spoke, and I had failed so utterly to get the men to put a brighter face on the affair, that I too began to make collar-work of it.

There was no doubt that everyone was getting to the end of his tether, and I hoped and prayed continually that the bivouac ground was not far off. We were cursed and exhorted by everybody. The colonel came and let fly, and I think I vaguely remember the brigade commander. Officers, non-commissioned officers and men were too dead beat to bare or take much notice; everyone was doing his level best, but the mood was wrong. Depression is as catching as exhilaration, and it does not leave a man so quickly, nor can it easily be thrown off. The psychology of mood is a deep study; the spirit and the body, supposed for centuries to be contrary one to the other, are, more truly, complementary and subject to profound interactions.

The spirit of the gallows hung over us as we neared, at about half-past seven, the cursed railway that reminded us of the other end of the march and consequently of the length of it. I remember noticing that the width of the rails was different from ours and seeing a small pile of sleepers and wishing I could steal them for a hut. And I remember helping men up the slight embankment and over the rails and making the wretched fellows form up on the other side. Then we started marching again, anyhow, over a sloppy barley field covered with stubble. The companies were now going separate; I was beginning to wonder where the bivouac ground would be, when I saw one of the other companies halting. Then I understood. It was here, in the sloppy field. I felt like a doomed person.

"Tomorrow," I reflected, "some of us will be very ill and some will be dead. What a rotten end—to die in a sodden barley field!"

But this black mood nobody guessed at, for I kept it to myself.

"Look here," I said in a low voice to the subalterns, when we had fallen the men out to do what they could for themselves. "This is pretty awful, but for God's sake don't let the men think so. What about getting them something to eat? Have you heard anything about rations?"

Temple, who looked white and ill and miserable, said:

"I'm awfully sorry, skipper, but I shall have to sit down"; and down he sat on his equipment, dropping it in the mud. "I don't think I shall be able to go on tomorrow," he added in a melancholy voice.

"Rot!" I said, as cheerfully as I could; "of course you will."

Trobus, a small person with tremendous self-confidence and with the bounce of a squash-rackets ball, was still ready for events. His vital spark was undimmed. And Jackson, older and harder and with a stubborn will accustomed to knock up against a rough world, was also determined to see things through.

A party was got to unload the Lewis-gun mules, and the men told they could put up their bivouacs. No tea was possible—no one had any dry wood; and the supply, camels were still far behind, their legs slithering outwards on the mud. The battalion as a unit could do nothing for its members: co-operative effort sank before the wet miseries of that cold, cheerless field. That most dismal provender, "the unexpended portion of the day's ration," was all that remained to warm the men's sopped bodies and to cheer their souls. Slowly they dragged their sheets out, and with cold fingers began buttoning them together. Every little movement was now a conscious one, and trivial things had to be got through by special efforts of the will and forced attention.

The "subconscious self," the skilful, silent worker that does so much without proclamation for all of us, jibs sometimes under adversity, ceases to be an automaton, and has to be tackled and brought under by a surprised and angry intelligence. But it is not her proper realm that Intelligence takes over on these occasions, and she stumbles, and swears, and makes mistakes, and rouses the passions. These come like a bursting-charge to finish the matter by explosion. Finally, at huge expense and loss of vital power, the button is buttoned or the knot untied.

It is better to carry on your back the sheet and stick that make your half of a single bivouac-tent than have it packed in a bundle and trusted to a train of mules. We had at least got the materials for erecting shelters, however soaked the ground underfoot might be. Once, in Macedonia, we had fallen into an even worse plight, for the mules, which then carried these sheets, did not arrive till the early morning, and many of the men spent the whole night in walking aimlessly up and down the field, trying to keep warm. I remember an occasion in that country when the bivouacs were unloaded on arrival and the men fell asleep, one after the other, while putting them up. A visitor coming at the first morning light, would have supposed we had all been struck dead in the act.

Exhaustion had not bowled them out so utterly this night; now they were up rather against positive affliction, discomfort, and the general wretchedness of things. As we strugglingly arrived it had appeared that they were finished, but the putting off of packs and equipment had liberated a few last ounces of energy they had been carrying, as it were, somewhere down in their boots. Painfully, mainly by the dogged energy of a few, the little gables rose again in the darkness and the cherished stumps of candles were relit.

To human beings squatting on their hunkers, trying with entrenching tools how far the mud goes down, nothing in the world matters but the solution of the problem in hand. They forget whether they are married or single, R.C., Presbyterian or C. of E., commissioned, non-commissioned or just simply "men." These acquired distinctions lose significance as elementary matters of self-preservation claim their entire attention. Their minds, contracted to a single point, revert to prehistoric excitements, such as scratching for a hole in the dry.

Lord Dunsany has expressed this concentration born of necessity, the being "up against it," the state of mind that exists when life holds few things and those simple and nasty, in a short play called *The Dog*. It has more of the innate misery and primitive savagery of war in it than all the objective studies this war has brought forth.

The men were helpful enough, ingenious, patient in adversity as they always are, miserable, but able to triumph to some extent over the evil conditions under which they laboured. They found by persistent scraping and contriving that it was possible to discover a fairly dry bed. The ground had been powdery on the top, but was hard underneath; the rain had not been falling long enough to penetrate the earth deeply; it was possible, once a bivouac had been pitched, to scrape most of the mud away. Their clothes were wet through and it was very cold, but that was ancient discomfort and could be put up with.

The officers, less accustomed to misfortune, bore the affair, I am sorry to say, more hardly, and with tempers more on edge. Everyone ticked everyone off: the wheels of our unit grated very badly. The subalterns in my company could not decide at first whether to join their sheets up to make one big bivouac or bivouac apart, or where exactly on the mud they should settle. They said bitter things to each other and accused one another of selfishness and other vices.

Finally, Jackson marched grimly off with his servant and became managing director of his own show, while Trobus and Temple, flung by Jackson's independence into each other's arms, made haste to make a better shelter than the man with whom they had quarrelled.

For me, I dwelt apart in lonely state, outside these wrangles, intervening only as a peacemaker, sometimes going so far as to take privately to task the man who was in the wrong. Beattie had laboured like the good soul he was, and I had crawled into my valise, when Tomboys, the signalling officer, put his head in and gave me the orders. He too was angry and dejected, and particularly wroth with the adjutant, who, it appeared, had been particularly wroth with him. From the sheaf of complaints, he emptied into my cold ear, it seemed that headquarters were about as amiable to each other as my own company staff.

Next day, a damp, tempestuous morn, all the officers were assembled before the C.O. and "ticked off" in merciless fashion. Whether the C.O. had himself been rated by the brigade commander and was passing it on, or whether he had merely concocted this mental julep for us during an uncomfortable night, I am unable now to determine. We all received his remarks in the wrong spirit and went away feeling hurt and rather rebellious.

Several of the companies, in spite of the efforts of the company commanders, who really had put their backs into it after the C.O.'s lecture, were late on parade, partly owing to the men, some of whom had removed their boots during the night and had great difficulty in getting them on again, and partly owing to the mules, who turned up long after time, caked all over with mud. My mare seemed to have been rolling during the night, and was ungroomed. I could imagine, from these signs, the frightful time Hoyle must have had, for he took a great pride in his animals, and would not, save in an extremity, have sent them in this state on to parade. "It can't be done" had proved actually true—he had been unable to "fulfil his obligations."

The column moved off somehow over the railway along a muddy track to find the starting-point and meet the rest of the brigade—moved with a sense of lateness and everything wrong, cursing because the rendezvous was so far away. Our night at Esdud, for it was near that historic spot we had encamped, had not been a success; the day before us looked hardly more hopeful.

Yet this inter-chapter upon rain can end on a pleasant note. Weather conditions in the East alter suddenly: Palestine is a land of quick changes, "from grave to gay, from lively to severe." We had not been marching long before the clouds cleared, and we found ourselves once again under a blue sky that looked as permanent as ever. The rain was over and gone, and though there were no singing birds in that bare place to cheer us, there was whistling in the ranks and a chorus or two, as in the old training days in England.

We were treated to such hearty melodies as "What cheer, the old brown jug, how *are* yer?"; "Oh farmer, have you a daughter fine?"; "Mop it down"; "We haven't seen the *Kaiser* for a *very* long time":—the last-named ending with the statement "He's the leader of a German band, and he ain't no cousin of mine."

By noon the plain had gone far towards drying, and the men, their spirits once again sky-high, were swinging along splendidly. We struck into a track that was almost a road, and this led us through a native village. There was a pool on the right and a tamarisk-tree and some plantations bordered with cactus, like those we had seen outside Gaza. We noticed some abandoned Turkish guns on the left. Native women and children, the former with matted hair, the latter little dirty gutter-snipes, stood and stared at us; the road twisted suddenly, and in a few moments, we had left it behind.

I seem to remember a place some distance away to the left, to which we never drew near—a place which boasted one or two houses with red-tiled roofs. But my memory breaks down about here, and there is nothing for it but to make a great skip to the evening camping place, a field very like the last, and again on the western side of the railway. Though the roads had dried during the day, this field was still as wet as an English plough-land after a night's rain. The men were pretty whacked on arrival, but not quite to the point of exhaustion. Moreover, we were drawing nearer to Jerusalem, had entered well into our adventure, and the interest roused at the start was beginning to return.

I well remember that on our arrival there was a slight uncertainty as to exactly how the field had been allotted and where the companies should halt. We were "messed about" a little in consequence, and I can see as clearly as if they were standing before me Tomboys and his weary signallers, who had come to rest in three separate places, and each time had been politely but firmly kicked out by one or another of the company commanders. This time we arrived in daylight, an advantage indeed. But night soon came, and I cannot for the life of me call to mind if it was here or on the wet bivouac of the night before that I bought a handful of oranges.

I had wandered about looking for wood, and met a woman and two children carrying oranges that looked green and tasted delicious. It was the first of many similar purchases in the days to come. I grossly overpaid the woman, giving her all my change. Yet she and her brats came whining after me. With tall words and threatening cutlass-like movements of a walking-stick, I drove them away.

Some kindly A.S.C. men sitting round a bonfire gave me wood: it must have been on this night that it happened. For wood means warmth and joy, and this bivouac was relatively a happy one. Xenophon, true campaigner that he was, never failed to make a note in his diary whenever he found wood. "*And there was wood on that stage.*" How the translation of it bored me at school! how little I guessed as a boy that I too would go on a campaign and have adventures! When things have gone wrong and everyone has grumbled, I have often thought of that wonderful Greek leader, who was not above getting up before his men and chafing their frostbitten feet.

After we were settled down, many wanderers from another battalion came into our lines in the darkness, dead-beat, asking for the whereabouts of their unit. That is the last thing I remember—those poor miserables. During the night everything dried up: next morning was radiant. The episode of the first rains was over. We were draggled, and tired, and dirty. But everyone was cheerful again, and after all we were still alive. It was a sober, chastened and thankful battalion that set out in the morning towards El Kustine.

3: AT EL KUSTINE

At El Kustine everything went well, and yet as I think of it, it brings back to me a sinking heart and a feeling of utter loneliness. The march, as usual, had been a long one, but neither so long nor so tiring as the two that ended miles from anywhere in the wet, desolate fields. This was not a mud village, like the one we had passed on the previous day, but a place of some importance, with a few houses of stone, and a proper water supply from carefully looked after wells. These houses were scattered and at some distance from us, but though we were camped on a field again, it was easily come-at-able—a piece of gentle up and down plain land on the immediate left of a good road. Moreover, we had arrived early, and had had plenty of time to make our arrangements for the night.

Though without incident, the march had not been without interest, for we had run at last into the back area of General Bulfin's corps, and buildings, men, and military material were frequent upon the way. I remember particularly a pretty building of light construction, put up for some military purpose by the Turk. It had been quickly turned to use, had become an engineering shop, and men were already busily overhauling two eighteen-pounders.

There was something more than a sigh of relief when we found that this time no intervening area of rain-soaked land separated us and the road from the place we were to rest in. Everyone was profoundly grateful, and hailed the slight tumulus on the left with positive enthusiasm. A good, dry, well-drained place, bare at the foot, where it flattened out invitingly for the companies now already contentedly pitching their bivouacs. The surrounding country did not interest us; the daylong march, the nightly encampment, had become so routinised, so much plain had been gazed on during the hours of movement, that rest found us with incurious eyes, going about our domestic affairs with the circumscribed fidelity of ants.

It was rumoured that here for several days we were to stay, a popular piece of gossip, for everyone was tired of the continual drive. We had arrived unusually early, and the irregular clusters of tents that marked each company ("gipsy encampments" an irritated staff officer had dubbed them on the Vardar) were rising at leisure to the accompaniment of fragments of witticisms, hurled like footballs from platoon to platoon.

Bilkins, a sergeant who without effort carried the hilarity of a n—r-minstrel corner-man into ordinary life, vocalised the general satisfaction by breaking out from time to time into remarks of extreme oddness and inappropriateness, such as: "Who says a nice chicken, now? Come along, boys, come along!" or "Canterbury lamb, all the very very very—that's a beautiful piece of meat, ma'am, you're looking at, straight from the fields of Sussex."

Somebody shouting "Anyone got a bit of string for my bivvy?" was instantly answered derisively, "Anyone got a loaf of bread?" that commodity being unknown; scraps of "Are you from Dixie?" whistled to the accompaniment of a universal driving-in of pegs, were perhaps marred, perhaps thrown into relief, by the voice of the orderly corporal, with his "Come along, those orderlies from number nine platoon." The glad announcement that "rations were up" caused at once a volley of questions as to whether it was dates or raisins. The creatures—change them now to bees—were obviously happy within limits: the hive gave forth a regular contented hum.

Small domestic affairs had occupied me as well as the others that first hour of our sojourn. I had chosen a place apart for my officers, and myself cleared a space slightly more remote than they were from the ruck of tents. At our back was an area where no one camped, for it was covered with long, dry stalks—of barley, I think. I at once began to collect these for my fire, while Beattie, who had already erected my bivouac, went hunting for stones, scarce in that field. Together we made a small fire-place, happy as boys on the spree, full of the spirit and youthful enthusiasm of Stevenson's lantern-bearers.

"Look," I said, "rations are up, Beattie; buck along and get ours, and tell the quartermaster-sergeant that I want a whole tin of cocoa, and won't draw again for a week. Take our cardboard box with you, or we shan't get our share of dates. Is it a jam-day? No? Well, I've got half a tin in reserve. We saved it at Gaza. Cut along."

Off the good henchman trotted, and I was left to myself. Restless ever, thoughts and responsibilities, now manual work and simple pleasures were over, came crowding back to knit the forehead. The march had gone fairly well, but one platoon had not been doing its best—the platoon that numbered amongst its men Egan and Thunder. There was a third fellow, too, Tom Peter, a butcher's boy from Tooting, who completed the trio. They all wanted a strong hand, but they were led by Trobus, a brave young rascal, who, amongst all his good qualities—and he was a great favourite of mine—remained unfortunately a boy.

All my officers, as I have remarked earlier in this history, were out-standing personalities, but Trobus had that special quality of bounce and resiliency that is often to be found in persons of small stature. To call him a cock-sparrow would be unkind, and perhaps libellous, but he had the supposed mental attitude of that bird towards the world. "A sporting youngster" is nearer to the mark.

His romantic past, which I have always envied, shows him to be made of something better than fustian. The beginning of the war found him at Sandhurst, but not for long, for he ran away and joined the ranks of a London unit, and became a sergeant or sergeant-major—I have never been quite clear which.

Dropped into my unloving arms from the skies, just as the bat-talion was leaving England for France, this stormy and independent babe had fought his way from unpopularity (a skin-deep affair) to general acceptance. He was always getting into rows, carried a stiletto for the adjutant, who had never learnt to love him, and was never happier than when he could display himself on somebody's horse when somebody was away.

A year earlier, on the Vardar, he had shown us, though proof in his case was not necessary, that he was of high courage and had streaks of a certain heroism, for though wounded in an appalling mix-up of his own devising when on a battalion patrol (which I had the pleasure of watching, standing on the top of the trenches clad in a suit of striped pyjamas), he told his tale afterwards very gamely before the colonel, and never let on that he was hurt.

Wonderful are the intricacies of character that wait to baffle the inquirer, and I, who started so confident, have long since given up all pretences to wisdom or clear sight in such difficult matters; but the game goes on and judgments continue to be passed. Very personal and private are the internal affairs of a company, the moral and intellectual side that constitutes its real life, and for which no handbook can ever possibly exist.

In France the constant change in personnel in infantry battalions allowed little permanence to those thousands of small social confederacies known as company messes, the "skipper" and his friends the subalterns. Many of these happy alliances of three to six officers existed only long enough to taste the joys of fellowship when the shell came or the "stunt" was ordered that scattered them for ever.

But in the battalion of which I speak, and especially in this company, our little society had hung jealously together for over two years—years to be counted as some twenty of ordinary companionship. How well we knew each other, we who had loved and hated, squabbled and made it up, led in the same hole together in so many corners of the earth! A few superficial changes had taken place before the beginning of the campaign, but the core remained true.

Coborne, welcomed soon after our arrival in France as one by nature born to our kinship, had faithlessly succumbed to the superior material attractions offered by the post of Lewis-gun officer, a job on his own, and a seat at headquarters mess amongst the *nabobs*, with whom we were always more or less seriously at war.

I like to imagine him as he used to appear in France when going on duty, at the entrance to my dug-out, very much dressed for the part, armed at all points, clad in a voluminous and skirty trench-coat which bulged and overflowed his equipment, and seemingly hung all over with murderous weapons. Above it a fresh boyish countenance, shyly conscious of the fun it was creating, told that war was an unpleasant tonic that had to be swallowed somehow. We had lost him, our serious boy, and Beersheba had cost us an older and more senior member of the council. And now we marched on with the remnants, again to be put to trial, the ultimate trio, Jackson, Temple, and Trobus.

The slackness of his platoon, the lack of discipline in it, the failure to bring entirely to heel those precious three, Egan, Thunder and Tom Peter, brought me to the conclusion, as I paced quickly up and down at the edge of the barley patch, that the time had come again to tick Trobus off. Some boys attract periodical whackings, some sick people require periodical doses of medicine, and I had come to find or imagine that young Trobus was also so fashioned. He had a kind of socialistic tilt and liked to find himself the centre of a small group of men, his admirers, to whom he would tell stories, reaping huge admiration thereby, somewhat after the manner of a Little Lord Fauntleroy.

He was popular, and liked, but at the expense of something common to both parties that ought not to have been sacrificed. There had been several of these private interviews between him and his company commander, walks on the other side of a hill, monologues in the darkness punctuated by his monosyllabic replies. We had communed oft, in France, in Macedonia. Even if they did him no good, they did neither of us any harm, for a person of his breeding and intellectual possibilities was too well-born and too sensible to be offended, while, if nothing else resulted, our common ideals at any rate became a little more clearly defined.

"Trobus, I want to see you for a few moments," I called out when the decision had been reached.

"Right-ho! skipper," and the little dapper figure jumped up from a tent and came towards me with great seeming pleasure and alacrity.

I am horribly nervous on these occasions, though no one has ever guessed it, and I now took a deep breath to inspire myself with more confidence.

"Look here, Trobus," I said, after we had removed ourselves sufficiently from the world and he had assumed a pleased, expectant attitude. "Your platoon marched absolutely rottenly today; I hope you don't think they were all right."

"Well, skipper, if you don't mind my saying so, I thought they came along rather well, except perhaps just at the end. But then everybody was knocked."

"There's no use talking about it; your gang of cutthroats think a mighty lot of themselves, and they sometimes behave like a perambulatorful of babies. Look at that great hulking chap Thunder, who pretended he couldn't carry his pack, and just look at Goodwin V. and the example he sets them. All over the place. Dressing bad. Not covered off, slouching along. Worst platoon in the company. And it's your platoon. What have you got to say about it?"

"Well, skipper, if you say it's like that, I suppose it is so, but they're all jolly good fellows, and I've been doing all I can to look after them."

"Assing along, telling tall stories to a sergeant, isn't looking after a platoon on the march. Do I ride at the head of the column doing damn all? O yes, you worked all right when I came round and dropped on you, but that isn't good enough. And then you go and do a damned sight too much and cosset them. Look at number ten. Of course, they detest Jackson, but he does manage to get them along when they're whacked. What the devil does it matter if the men like you or not now?

"They like the fellow in the end who pulls them through and drops on them occasionally. Of course, there are ways of doing it. I wish to Heaven, Trobus, you'd begin to grow up. I don't mean intellectually—you and I can discuss poetry together in the mess, and the other fellows are out of it—but in the general conduct of things. Sight too much of the theatrical business, you know. I know you've been away on this ridiculous gas course of yours, but it's time you pulled the platoon together And then, you're always scrapping with Temple.

Do you want to go to another company?"

"You know I don't."

"Sometimes I don't believe you care much. I want to make you a bit more serious. This is all very nice and pleasant: certain amount of grub, some water—not enough to wash with, but still, some—nice fields, stalks to burn, rain all over, and Jim Morrow going back to rail-head and perhaps further to buy cigarettes and bring up spare clothing. We may stay here tomorrow or we may not. At any rate, it will only be another march, and the men can stick that; in fact, they'll jolly well have to. But do you think for a moment that this happy little pilgrimage is going on for ever?"

"I hope not, skipper," said Trobus piously.

"What I mean is that the thing's got an object, something's going to happen. We are thinking too much of condensed milk and who's got the largest share of jam. That's why I smashed the mess up. All these petty things. . . . It's enough to make a man—a *man*, Trobus—rather sick. My dear chap, what does anything matter except the job in front of us? Do you know where we are going?"

"Everyone's got a pretty good idea that we're going to Jerusalem."

"Well, it'll be a job, and it's time everyone began to brace themselves up for it. Palestine's one of the most difficult countries to fight in in the world. This plain will turn into a sea of mud directly those infernal rains start again. Judaea's a kind of slag-heap, all messed up with volcanic rocks, and the Jordan Valley, if any of us ever get there, is absolute hell. How they are going to feed us if we do take Jerusalem—that's what I'm thinking about. And it'll be darned cold, too. I don't suppose Pat Egan, that skrimshanking light-weight of yours, would be very enamoured of what's before him if he could project his grousing little mind into the future. You know what we shall be up against. It's up to you to think about it occasionally."

"Do you think we are in for a pretty thick time? Don't you think the old Turk'll pack up when he sees us coming?"

"It depends on whether he sees your platoon or not. But, absolutely seriously, do try and put some more guts into it, and get your N.C.O.'s to do some work for you. Now, Temple has worked that sort of thing to a fine art; in fact, he overdoes the delegating business. I wish you and he could pool qualities. By the way, are you trying for a job at the division as O.C. gas-masks?"

"Well, of course, skipper, I should be awfully sorry to leave, but I am keen on getting a show of my own."

"So's everyone. Now understand. While you're here you've got to put your little back into it. Right?"

"I will try to remember what you have said."

Thus, the demure youngster and the close of the episode.

I hate playing the heavy father, and did not feel victorious as we strolled back to the camp. Just before we parted I was smitten with contrition.

"Come round and feed in my bivouac," I said. "I've got some boiled rice and heaps of sugar. Beattie does rice beautifully."

He hesitated.

"Temple and I have got a feed on; we're doing our figs in a new way. If you don't really mind. Thanks awfully, you know. Come round to us."

I decided to feed alone.

As darkness fell over El Kustine shrouding the open plain, shutting out the sight of a white house and the curving line of a road, fencing off each cluster of dim-lit bivouacs from the other, contracting our horizons until we hardly moved or speculated beyond the limit of a neighbour's tent-pole, a feeling of extreme loneliness came upon me and made me long for society. The excitement of the day's march, the necessity of looking after the company, so many men to talk with, the old business of arranging things upon arrival, generally left me in the evening sleepy, unspeculative, and contented. Lying at full length in the combined shelter shared by Temple and Trobus, or paying a visit to the sometimes solitary Jackson, a little desultory talk in the cool dark would pleasantly end the day.

Great our common store of reminiscence, many a tale at these impromptu meetings would be dug up and retold with all the detail the two or the trio could provide. None of us cared so much for the tale as a tale; it was the going over again of the past that allured us and made the silent ones happy and quiet in their listenings. Soldiers all down the ages have loved to meet round camp fires and recall old adventures, and Tacitus in his *Agricola* has a delightful passage where he makes the Roman rank and file, camped somewhere up in Scotland, boast and tell stories to each other of the old high times they had in Germany and Gaul.

Sometimes we would speak of the poor old ship that took us from Marseilles to Salonica, and sigh over the great luxurious saloon ("*and all the food in her,*" quoth Temple) lying a-tilt at the bottom of the Mediterranean, with the fish darting like quick shadows in and out of the portholes. Again, the beacon-fires of wild Mahmudli would guide us down from the mountain passes on the most savage of nights, when I cut down a tree on arrival, in a kind of wild attempt to show that we were not "done in." Some could go back as far as that misery of snow on Salisbury Plain when we were penned in rows of horrid hutments, each with its ugly centre-swung skylight and bulb of naked light.

But I was the only one (unless Coborne looked in upon us for the sake of old acquaintance) who could recall the high adventures of the Essex campaign, what time the division got first upon its myriad legs—all we endured those days through lack of knowledge. There was the bombing of number sixteen platoon and the mules, on our disastrous trek to the Vardar, and those funereal patrols on the down-lands in front of the trenches. Pleasant tales, too: bathes in Lake Arzan, the white stripped figures against the low red cliffs at her margin, and memories of the deafening noise that comes from millions of froggy throats at night.

But no inheritance of scenes remembered came this night to charm me from myself. I was alone. The subalterns were eating their dinners happy in the usual trivialities of talk: I had finished mine, and did not want to join them. A tired loathing had taken possession of me; I wanted to forget them all for a while, I wanted change. "To how many more places," I pondered, "shall I have to drag these weary men, how many more fields wait the coming of our bivouacs?"

Imagination, reaching backward over this idea, brought no pleasant pictures to the inward eye; I saw instead columns of dark figures, concentrating on roads, coming on to hillsides, unpacking, packing, endlessly marching on. They kept no certain step, there was no vigour in them, or purpose, or healthy glow; they were prosecuting a task without a meaning; it once had a meaning, but they had forgotten what it was. Even the reality that lay before me now merged into my shadow-world and became thin and cold and unsuggestive. Thoughts that did not get anywhere, that started no *vistas* of enjoyment, led to no desire for action, happened and shrivelled within me, like dead things perishing off a tree.

I was not so much "fed up," to use the good slang phrase that covers the soldiers' malady, for fed-upedness (the word is no new coinage) carries a slight tone of anger and annoyance about it; I was suffering from shrunken heart, the sad eye turned upon itself, the nasty, un-escapable spectacle of my own unlovely ego. This is the mood that drives a man forth to batten upon his fellows. It drove me out of the camp, over the hill, to stumble in strange lines in search of I did not quite know what. "I will go,' I thought, "to see the field ambulance." After much searching, I found them, hung about outside their tents, and finally hurried away without seeing anybody.

Five minutes' wandering brought me to a row of guns—eighteen-pounders, that had supported us in France. Here was a chance of a jolly evening; I would look up the gunner officers, go and have a drink with Blaine or Moyton, and talk of the days when, doing duty as observation officers, they used to share my deep dug-out in the Bonnal, the old French trench that formed our bit of the line. Led by the light of a bonfire, I went expectantly forward to where an old buck-sheet stretched over two wagons did duty for their mess. There was a table under it—they had actually got a table!—but an orderly, coming forward to meet me, said that mess was over, and "Captain Blaine and Mr. Moyton, sir, have gone to the brigade." I hung there talking with him, and then, tired of his conversation, plunged back into the darkness. What would one have given at that moment for ten minutes of home, in England!

The fireside, books in a study, the red-bricked path leading to the door. Take a deep breath, steady yourself, and knock. Your mother herself opens it. "My *dear*, and you *never* said you were coming." "No, it's a real surprise."

O, come up! What's the order of march tomorrow? D—C—B—A. Let's think of the sergeants. There's that tall fellow Challard. Damn it, I can see him going home too. Tomorrow we shall move on again. And every mile we go we've got to march back. Unless . . . mustn't think of that. At any rate, there's work to be done tomorrow. A sobering thought, good quench for the imagination. Slowly, as I plodded back to the isolated bivouac, ideas of duty rose steadily uppermost. Without knowing why or how, the mysterious ship that is me, going in darkness on the ocean of Time, righted. Everyone else, sensible, ordinary fellows, had gone to sleep. Jackson was snoring like a grampus.

I stole over to look at him—he was lying like a bundle of old clothes, and it was difficult to see which was head or tail. Trobus was flat on his back. Temple had gone to sleep like a babe, one hand stretched out, with the palm open. I stood looking at them for a moment, thought of all the good work they had done for me, cursed myself for a silly, self-centred maniac, snuggled down into my own valise, and went straight into the land of dreams.

CHAPTER 3

The Hills of Judaea

1: WE LEAVE THE PLAINS

Though it had at first been supposed that at El Kustine we were destined for a time to come to anchor, the morning after our arrival saw the usual preparations for going ahead. At first, we were both tired and sorry. The battalion was getting rather exhausted by its wanderings, and though the place had nothing to offer but a well-drained piece of camping ground by a roadside, it was sufficient to content most who, like the sea-weary mariners in *The Lotus-eaters*, had had enough and to spare of travel. Yet as each company turned on to the road with its train of mules and, with a preliminary change or two of step, got into the old rhythm and felt the hard stones under its heavy tread, spirits rose, Kustine was forgot, and everyone began to sniff the air and look for such adventure as might befall.

The setting out marked somehow a turning-point in the history of our late travels, and we were conscious of the fact. In the beginning uncertain plans and counsels had caused us to veer upon the plain: the sails of our good ship had flapped a little in that indeterminate time; no strong motive had existed to act as a breeze to bear us easily along. Then rumour, blowing around us, though it inspired us at intervals, came with no set purpose to drive us on our course. But now reliable news had arrived, and its tonic influence drove us with fresh energies upon our way. Jerusalem-wards! Out of the plain and on to the hills of Judæ, unto which, so soon, we should be lifting up our eyes!

That Jerusalem was to be visited by us in the guise of liberators was an idea now handed freely about from man to man: it was known as a certainty that the goal of all these marches was the Holy City. This, with the talk of the hills and knowledge that we were coming

68

into changing country, leaving the old monotony of the plains behind, woke us up and made us look about with fresh enthusiasm, new comments, forward desires. The men were cheerful and chatted easily. The careless platoon, which had apparently had some of my remarks to Trobus passed on to it, was marching with a fine don't-care air, touched with lately re-established pride.

There was general speculation about the Holy Land, but talk ran chiefly on the hills. They made us feel a little nervous. Report said that it was cold up there. "Regular mountains" a chance-met returning warrior had called them: "A hell of a country" another had flung over his retreating shoulder as we passed. We heard that there were stones on them, in appalling numbers. Thoughts turned naturally to Macedonia: no one wanted to have those experiences over again.

Whatever they would be like, they would be strange, the routine of the past fortnight would be broken: we might even have to march in single file. And some, meditating this, called back for us in few and vivid sentences our corkscrew ascent of the heights beyond Snevce, when, if you raised your eyes, you could see our thin toiling column repeated four or five times in the heights above, as it wound this way and that, at last to disappear round the topmost corner.

The last miles of plain country were not to pass away with nothing for the eyes to gaze on; we had not marched far before we came upon fresh evidence of the Turks' retreat. Here was a railway line and a station and smashed houses, and a girder-bridge, badly damaged. The chief thing I noted as we passed was the skill with which the Turks had rendered the railway useless. At first sight it appeared to be intact: a great haul, I thought, for there was some rolling-stock on it at places; but looking more closely, I discovered that every other rail had neat little holes blown out of it, each break diagonally opposite the two on the other side of the line. Thus, the entire railway was rendered absolutely useless for a long time to come. Many captured stores were lying about, and there was a broken aeroplane—rare object on this front.

Passing amongst this debris we came to some uneven country, and had ten minutes' halt near a fair-sized pool which lay next to the great circular tank of a pumping-station. There were black objects in the water, which looked thick and dirty and was covered with scum, and I saw with surprise that they were the carcases of a herd of fine dark-coloured oxen, slaughtered that they might not fall into our hands, and flung there to contaminate the water. The pumping plant was broken up, and all the water in the cistern had been fouled. It seemed that the

Turks had not been in quite such a hurry on this occasion, and had been able to do their work of destruction well.

The earlier stages of this long march are dim in my memory, which has preserved only pictures of certain stretches in it, some incidents, and a sense of its colour and feeling tone. There is a vignette of a group of Turkish prisoners, little men, with dark hair, brown skins and ugly ears, working on the road near the fouled pond, and guarded by an unnecessary number of our men. I next see the column racing over some open country, bad ground to march on, full of twists and turns and places where the mules had to fall behind the companies. The brigade staff had the direction of the march in hand, and us, unfortunately, in tow, and so absorbed was the brigade commander in affairs of his own—probably in finding the exact route we were to take—that he and his people went too fast for the unfortunate infantry following in his wake.

The distance between the companies widened and widened until they marched as separate units; the mules, which had waited for us to pass, made desperate efforts to catch up; everyone became angry and annoyed. The colonel, lithe figure lightly equipped, riding up and down the column on a little horse, did what he could to put matters right. I pitched my woe at him as he passed, and suggested the brigade should have their attention called to what was happening. The pointed red pennon carried by the brigade commander, the flag we had learnt to follow in two countries, was bobbing gaily ahead, and we began to curse it bitterly as a thing we were tacked on to and which didn't care tuppence for the shortness of our legs.

I have often wondered if our leader knew the consuming interest with which, towards the end of a march, or even during the progress of it, we used to watch the movements of that directing flag. For where it was planted, there we rested the night. Its departure from the road up a hillside or into a field was followed with eager anxiety. Was he going to stop at last, did he like that bit of ground, or would he rove further on? With exactly the same feelings, asking the same question, yeomen and peasants of ancient times followed at the heels of their lord's banner. The Turks go to war with numbers of flags; we are less picturesque: the red pennon was our only standard; we have followed it hundreds of miles like straining dogs.

We picked up when we came to the road, and good-humour was restored. A long period of marching followed, hour after hour, over open country which yet, surely enough, was steadily on an upward trend. The weather was as cloudless as the day before, very hot, but not oppressive. The prevailing tint of the country was still the red-brown to which we had become by this time well accustomed. At the halts we were now solicited by sellers of nuts and oranges, commodities that frantically eager natives dressed in all sorts of robes and odds and ends of clothing, hauled about on their shoulders in sacks. The men were as eager to buy as the natives were to sell, but there was a great shortage of cash, and they did not understand Egyptian paper money, the soldiers' chief currency.

Nevertheless, there was great crowding round the vendors, and in the interests of discipline officers had to allow a certain number of men from each platoon to buy for the others. The bargaining was an amusing affair, for neither side knew a single word of the other's language. You showed a coin, and then indicated by the holding up of fingers the number of oranges you expected to get in exchange. A more popular method was to take the oranges, and continue taking them until the owner closed up his sack angrily and began to move away. Then he was entreated by many English slang words and much pantomime (including whistling as to a dog) to return, and business was reopened.

By these and similar methods a rough rate of exchange was arrived at. Both sides were frequently swindled in the process. I remember now that there was one word common to both parties— "*backsheesh*"—of which the men made great comic use to get extra oranges when everything else failed. So ingrained in the Eastern mind is the idea of "*backsheesh*," that they yielded to the suggestion, even when made against themselves. They probably made huge profits on every transaction, for oranges are so cheap in Palestine as almost to be given away.

But they certainly made no profits on some deals that came off later, when we were at rest at Latrun, but which may well be told of here. By that time the men, though well supplied with paper money, had spent their cash. This paper money of ours the natives still regarded with great suspicion. Egyptian notes, while of considerable artistic beauty, are not of striking appearance or gaudy in colour: one reason, possibly, why they did not appeal to the Palestinians.

Suddenly a humourist thought of turning their ignorance, suspicion, and crude taste to account. He managed to pull from one of the ration jam tins a highly coloured and elaborately printed label. He then took it to an old fellow with a sack of oranges, and by signs and gestures gave him to understand that this note was of such high value and rarity that it would buy up all the others. He took the bait, and a certain company had an unwonted feast.

The afternoon was half worn through when the country began to be sufficiently broken to indicate that we were now traversing those miles which, though not yet running through hill-land, had left the plain behind. The road's long ribbon, usually laid out in clear stretches before us, now suffered frequent derangement and lay in kinks and turns. The fields on either side, contoured like the partially closed palm of a hand, or again, as the hollows gave place to rising ground, like the convex back of one, showed that we were drawing near to the last gentle upheavals of a region of old volcanic disturbance. The land was being cultivated, right up to the roadside in many instances, and we passed ploughs at work—primitive instruments, yoked to oddly paired animals, such as a bullock and a small donkey.

Dulled and wearied by the long monotonies of our wanderings in the plain, this sight of a changing landscape cheered us mightily. Before many minutes had passed, we had drawn near to ground that was covered with stones, and we noticed a small outcrop of rock in a piece of land that nevertheless had been scratched by the plough.

Gradually we passed into a diversity of types of ground: one field would have lovely soil, with hardly a stone on it; the next would be peppered all over with bits of rock; a third would be fairly good; then would begin a small area of native hill-country, gentle of slope as yet, but with all the features that we were to know later in vastly more accentuated forms, country where rock held dominance, and herb and thorn and drifts of soil tried vainly to cover it.

Here was the beginning of the true Palestine, the rocky outskirts of Judaea, the land of the New Testament. There was hardly a man in the ranks who did not notice these things. The same sentences ran in the heads of all: *A sower went forth to sow. And as he sowed, some seeds fell by the wayside . . . and some fell upon stony ground—and some fell upon good ground. . . .* Memory, sadly rusted, could not deliver the parable entire. How often in churches in England had the perfect teaching fallen upon our staled ears!

And now—why, the thing was true! Here, at any rate, the natural side of the picture was displayed before us in realistic detail. We were not as travellers, eager after reading and preparation to test and prove; the wonderful truth of description had taken us by surprise. Very few at this moment seemed the years that had elapsed since Christ walked in Judaea, very new and unproven our Empire and the civilization for which it stood. The types of ground with their ill and good and indifferent responses and the hearts of men they served to illustrate, both existing now as then, produced this feeling of the illusion of time.

It was borne home to us as no argument could that the New Testament was not "made up." The elements of which Palestine is made are few, simple, and vivid. It is a bare, uncompromising country, with a direct, severe appeal. It is painted in its literature with extraordinary truth—a truth that makes Oriental fables seem false, eccentric, and flaccid. Here, where the ground had to be worked upon devotedly before it would yield a harvest, everything had a meaning. These were some of the thoughts that held us as we marched.

The road, which was now rising, took a turn to the left as it passed over the top of the hill, and now the red pennon thought it would take a short cut. Soon we were struggling along, our ranks broken, among the rocks we had lately been discussing. The pace was quick; it was as much as we could do to keep up. This was more like Macedonia again. We were cursing the pennon, which seemed so utterly thoughtless of the pains and troubles of burdened foot-soldiers, when, to our relief, it bobbed down onto the track; we scrambled after, and then there came a halt.

The first foretaste of the hills now gave place to sweeping ploughlands. This was fertile country. To right and to left nothing greeted our eyes but open fields. The road, a straight track, entered upon a slow descent. We settled down to face the last stages of the march. It was now very late in the afternoon; we had been going since morning; the distance, greater than we had ever compassed on previous marches, was beginning to tell. The cooler air, the interest provided by the new landscape, knowledge of the purpose of the march, had so far kept fatigue in abeyance.

A place called Latrun was to provide us a bivouac ground; conversation about it, estimation of its distance, now began, even as it had begun when we were on our way to Louez, marching one late afternoon along the Arras road on our first journey to the line in France. Well do I remember how painfully those last hours dragged, how silently and automatically the men plodded along. At length, topping a slight rise, we saw in the distance in front of us the veritable hill country—mountains we should have called that tumbled mass, had not the Bulgarian frontier revised for good our idea of what a mountain is. Down at the foot of those dark hills some buildings lay—they seemed just to the left of the road on which we were marching. Some formed at once a wild hope of billets. All supposed that we should march straight to the village.

Estimates had varied as to the distance of the place that lay before us; it was soon proved that they all erred on the side of nearness. Three-quarters of an hour still saw us a considerable distance away. More details were now visible. We could see that our road, now on a gradual descent, bore slightly to the right, leaving our supposed destination well to the left. On the right, in some low open fields just where the hills began, a house stood, with three poplar-trees near it, and something that looked like a well.

We now transferred our longing hope to this piece of territory. At this moment our advance officer, the indefatigable Coborne, who had been forward with the staff captain choosing bivouac areas, trotted up on a horse, and was at once besieged with questions by the officers: "Where on earth is this place of yours?" "How much further have we to go?" "Is there any water?" "Is it anywhere this side of those trees?" But I demanded, of special right—for had he not been one of my own subalterns?—first and particular information, and drew him away and said:

"Can you point out exactly where the place is? The men are in the usual state. I hope it is not very far. We are absolutely whacked."

"It's rather difficult; but look here, do you see that brown patch?"

"What, right beyond the trees, ever so far?"

"Yes, it's a good long way. Two miles. These hills are frightfully deceptive. Well, it is past the patch, second to the right. You can't see it from here."

"Good Lord! Why on earth did you go so far?"

"The staff captain chose it. There's a stream. The brigade's all along it, on both sides."

"Thank heavens for the stream, anyway. Goodbye. See you later. I suppose you're pretty done in, yourself."

He rode away, to fall into the hands of others, and presently the column moved on. And now, when the first of those two miles had been accomplished, we noticed that the red pennon had moved to the side of the road. This bucked everybody up, for we knew that the brigade commander had drawn aside with his staff to watch us go by, a certain sign that the end of the march was at hand. The word was passed down. Company commanders spoke a word or two to their men. Sergeants, long dormant, asserted themselves. There was a general brisking up, a changing of step here and there, the reestablishment of sections of fours that had partly dropped back or pushed forward into spaces that belonged of right to those ghostly emptinesses known as "blank files," the men in general put on a better face and tried to pretend that they were not tired.

As we marched past, the general spoke to some of the company commanders, a formal remark perhaps, expressive of an assumed cheerfulness our hearts found no echo to, but valued, as coming from our chief. Then we passed him, and our thoughts turned again to the bivouac ground. The white road bifurcated where the hills began, a shoulder of rocky upland diverting it half left and half right, something like the top of a capital Y. The clustered buildings we had seen lay to the left: our road, which led past the solitary building and the three poplar-trees, slanted to the right.

At the parting of the ways a great block of traffic hindered our progress, which had been checked before owing to a returning ambulance convoy which pushed past us while we were half-across a narrow bridge; A military policeman, the first we had seen for a long time, stood endeavouring, without much success, to direct the mass of men and vehicles passing or stuck before him. A native cart, broadly made and drawn by oxen, contributed to the confusion. Commanders of units, as well as the men who composed them, were dog-tired, and very exasperated at being thus held up within sight of rest. Everyone knew the advantage of getting in before dark.

By slow degrees we pushed up the road, our field ambulance beside us, with all its array of sand-carts, wagons, and camels. We had all quarrelled in turn with the policeman, whom the commanding officer of the battalion in rear of ours had ridden forward especially to curse; I now witnessed a sharper disagreement. We had come to the place where we had to bear off to the right, come to it, too, just after a long train of camels belonging to another ambulance had started to cross our path, moving very slowly. Into this column some ambulance camels moving on our right now cut, dividing it in half. Up rode the captain in charge, full of injury, threatening reports and complaints.

Our captain, who had got the support of one of the brigade staff, politely damned him to blazes, and all the time kept urging his camels on. I do not know how it ended, but it enabled us and the camels to slip through. Everyone was bucked by the spirit shown by our ambulance, a very popular unit in the brigade, and cursed and scowled at the other for daring to want to get to its destination in advance of us.

Cross roads in the Judaean Hills

Now we were moving slowly along a beaten track of earth. Plough-lands of a rich chocolate brown rose on our right and merged into rocky uplands; over our left shoulder we could catch a glimpse of the road we had lately left, curving up between two great hills Jerusalem way. Slightly below us, to our right, and fringing the track we were treading, a ditch about six yards wide, full of reeds and grasses, held at the bottom a trickling stream of precious water. What it meant to us no one who has not travelled in the East can tell. The sharp and sudden interval of the early rains had long been forgotten. The mind's eye, gazing upon the past, roamed in remembrance over long stretches of sun-baked plains.

Twice the cliffs of a great chalk-cut *wadi* showed at the lowest places in their beds, small turbid pools of liquid very different from the joy of a freshly running stream. Save for these, and the vision of a well or two, nothing so refreshingly English as these grasses had been seen by us since our departure from our own country, more than two years ago. In Egypt we had seen no running water at all, though Timsah's lake at Ismailia, the French town on the canal, had been pleasant enough; our last sight of it had been a small river, waded across at dawn when we were on the way to the Vardar Valley, after a night of complicated misfortune the battalion will never forget.

The track was wide, the column had split up, and companies were in some instances marching abreast. Each commander was anxious to know where in this pleasant resting-place his lines would chance to be. I had cocked my eye at a good flattish piece of ground about a hundred yards further on, and on the left, when Coborne, whom I had met an hour or so back, up the road, came hurriedly towards me. "Your company's to go over there, skipper," he said, pointing across the rush-choked ditch to a steep sloping field of scanty proportions, littered with pieces of rock, "but you haven't got all of it. It is rather difficult to explain."

I boiled with indignation.

"What, that beastly place! You've had all this country to choose from, and you mean to say you've chosen *that!* It's impossible to get one company in—let alone two. And how are we going to get the mules across the ditch? Nice sort of a bivouac to come to after a fifteen-mile trek. I should think it's the beastliest bit of rocky waste in Palestine."

"I can't help it. There it is. The staff captain chose it. It isn't as bad as it looks, when you get over there."

"No, I expect it's a damn sight worse. Why on earth did you put anyone on that miserable spot?"

"The staff captain wanted everyone to be near the stream, so the companies had to go both sides, because of room."

There seemed some sense in that, and there was no use yelping at a thing done. We beat the rushes down and scrambled somehow into the gully and out on to the other side. The mules put their backs up at it, and had to be unloaded on the track. The actual channel where the water ran was about two yards wide. The water looked clean and good for drinking. The ground was as hard as nails, and covered with bits of rock, but the men soon set to work to roll them away. I got a party together and filled it with enthusiasm for a causeway across the stream, and in a few minutes a chain of men were rolling boulders into it, with schoolboy glee.

Meanwhile the subalterns had clambered up the steep side of the mountain under whose flank we were bivouacking, and had found a narrow but fairly flat ledge, on which a kind of rough grass mixed with prickly thistles was growing. From it one could see the whole brigade, the mule-trains still arriving, camels with their blue-smocked native attendants, the sand-carts of the ambulance with their wide iron tyres, made to take wounded across the desert and still taken with us in the advance. The sun was getting low, the hills that lay around us cast great banks of shadow on the plough-lands between them. Fires were lit down below where the transport had settled. The scene was full of beauty, and peace and content entered into our souls.

The wandering division had reached the hills of Judaea. Perhaps, ere the final effort, it would be given a rest. There were some who thought of the world's most peaceful poem, the lovely psalm where God is spoken of as a shepherd, leading His human flock "*beside the still waters.*" All felt that they had come to a haven, a place to lie down in and take a little ease. Like the Jews of old, we lifted up our eyes unto the hills, and found comfort in them.

2: AT LATRUN

To saddle the mules again and take you straightway up that winding mountain road to Jerusalem would spoil the proportions of the story I have to tell. For though our minds meditated during the next few days on the further travels and adventures that lay before us, leading our conversation from time to time upon the sights that waited beyond the turn of the road, our bodies nevertheless were most evidently at

Latrun, taking rest and drinking deep of comfort and delight. To miss out so delicious an interlude because you who have not been with us want to hurry on and get to the fighting would be unfair to those of the original adventurers who remain, and who have their own idea of how a tale ought to be told. I hold to the old method, pleasing to children, that lets no recallable jot or tittle escape, so that it contribute to what parliamentary committees call "the terms of reference."

How we marched to Jerusalem includes (the genius and the mortal instruments in counsel together have decided) accounts of rests by the way. Good Lord! there has been fighting enough in this war: none of us who have been through it are overanxious to get to the bloodshed. Buccaneers are not for ever sinking ships and pegging out their prisoners on desert strands; they are forced to careen sometimes, I am told, and get fresh water in little kegs, and look to what an army would call "interior economy." That is the time when the wild fellows, falling into a softer mood, write letters home to wives and sweethearts, very careful, all the same, not to mention the name of the island.

Flinty Dick goes off to buy oranges. Much good-natured swindling with the natives follows. The crew (our rank and file) mend their socks or cobble up their clothing. There is domesticity even in the life of soldiers on a campaign. Apollo is not for ever bending his bow. And yet, when pens and cameras and returned warriors have done their best, it is difficult, so fearful are the quick sympathies of those who perforce remain behind, to convince them that we do not use cold steel daily, or kill men as a matter of course every forenoon before we have our dinner.

Shortly after our arrival, and before the sun went down, I clambered off up the hillside on a private expedition. I was off to get fuel, stealing a march on the others. The good Beattie, left to clear a site for my bivouac at one end of the ledge mentioned in the last chapter, had not much of a nose for such things. I was at one time famous for my winnings and my scroungings, greatly to the annoyance of a former commanding officer, who was pleased to regard me as a thief, and I now turned this useful vice to account.

All good soldiers have a natural eye for fuel, fodder, and food, the three "f's" that nurture an army. The fiftieth part of a bully-beef case is not much to do one's cooking on; I like a cheerful blaze, and plenty of it. The ledge above ours was wider, but as barren. A sideways scramble up over loose rocks and low prickly thorn brought me to an unexpected field, almost flat, very stony, but covered with a sparse array of the dry stalks of some cereal.

Full of the pleasure of exploring, I took a good look round. Our own camp was now invisible below me, for the hill was very steep, but the height at which I stood gave me a splendid view of the summits that lay before us. I was looking eastward, towards the direction of Jerusalem, but no buildings could be seen except a few stone houses on the left of the Jerusalem road, built on a rocky slope that became finally the wedge of land that caused the road by which we had arrived to split into two. On the other side of this wedge, hidden from sight, lay Latrun. The whole of the view westwards was shut out by a wall of rock, sheer in some places, but with ways up it. Neither our own ledge nor this field now took the sunshine, which still washed the further slopes on the other side of the rivulet and made the Jerusalem road stand out in all its dusty white.

Again, these spaces of light and shadow took me back to my first position in the line in Macedonia, where, owing to our unfortunate position on the western side of a hill, the sun did not rise for my company until it had gilded two unworthy bodies of troops to the eastward for a good three-quarters of an hour. How different life on the plain, where everyone could see, first the saffron beginnings of the dawn, then the sympathetic western reflections of it, finally the yolk-red edge of the naked disc moving perceptibly up!

The dry stalks amongst which I stood would make fuel if sufficient were collected, but I determined to go further and look for something more solid. There might be a lump of wood higher up. Using a goat-track that led up the rock, I came upon a nest of straw, made in the hollow of a rock, and following along round it, discovered a natural store-house with a very narrow entrance, with plenty more, lying about on the floor. It looked clean and good, and I determined to have some to lie upon that night. A short climb took me over the rock's face, and I found myself on the large rounded summit of a hill, whose highest point was several hundreds of yards away.

Clumps of close-growing green prickly thorn (surely of this Christ's crown was made), small patches of mountain grasses, bare tables of slippery rock and a multitude of herbaceous plants of all kinds made up the surface of this height, and there were in places drifts of very rich black mould, that looked worth carrying away to form small artificial plots. Some distance to my left something appeared that kept my curiosity alive. It seemed as if the rocks had been fashioned by hand. On the way I passed a shallow well, cut in the solid rock and perfectly dry, the work of shepherds, no doubt. The square places amongst the rocks that had attracted me turned out to be store-houses for grain, partly made by rolling roughly-hewn stones together, partly by improving natural cavities.

Except for a small heap of grain at the far end of one of them and a heap of dried camel-dung at the entrance of another, they were all empty. Ancient places, I thought, unchanged perhaps since Abraham's times; and I stood for a moment, feeling for the first time the sense of being in a country which has remained unchanged throughout all history—the sense of the past, of being an intruder, a person come by accident on to a place where the simplest operations of agriculture (to use an absurdly modern word) were routinized before Western civilizations began. Such thoughts required no effort and came naturally enough to a solitary wanderer, glad to escape temporarily from the calculations and distresses of his own age and let imagination browse.

The wooden arm of a broken plough recalled the original purpose of my explorings and set me hurrying back with it. It was all I had been able to find; we had struck as woodless a spot as I had ever seen. The barley stalks, if barley had grown there, would make the best fire; I was soon back on the plateau, busy in their collection.

These, and my piece of wood, with straw for a bed and the results of Beattie's clearing of the ledge also to feed the fire, were material enough for a pleasant evening. Natives had come with nuts and oranges and were squatting in a line on the other side of the stream. The rations had been brought over the small stone bridge we had made. The water had been certified fit for drinking. That important matter of a boundary had been decided upon after embassies had come from the companies on my left and right; stones, the most ancient way of marking out territory, had been set up to prevent subsequent disputings. Headquarters, situate round the shoulder of our hill about a hundred yards to our right, had, with their usual energy, actually contrived—they were on softer ground—to dig themselves a mess. Fires were started; we mealed and were happy.

Orders came out early—a great bliss: there were to be no parades on the morrow; companies were vaguely ordered to bestir themselves in the ever-urgent matter of "interior economy." For one day, at all events, we were to rest; of a move there, was not the slightest sign. In the blessed peace of that first evening at Latrun I conceived a new dish, oranges stewed in sugar. It took all I had saved for several days past, and was an utter failure.

Next morning, we learnt that we were to stay at Latrun for several days. Parades were impossible on the piece of ground on which we lived, and, with the exception of a few domestic marshallings and the usual fatigues, the men's time was their own. Some of the officers from headquarters mess explored Latrun, returning with flat cakes of native bread, some of which was pressed on me with the encouraging remark that it was really not so bad when you had got used to it. But most of us rarely left our respective ledges, where we lay basking in the sun at midday while our servants washed our shirts in copper pots.

There was much lazy talk of Jerusalem, and some of us, on the off-chance, and in defiance of maps, climbed to the rounded top of the hill against which we lived, in the fantastic hope of catching a distant view of it. We only saw a confusion of magnificent hills and the great shadows cast by them on the plough-lands of Latrun, but the view westward crowned the pleasure we gained from the climb. Now we could look back for the first time upon the plain we had struggled over so long, all the brown expanse of it, and looking slightly northward see, with a strain of the eyes, Jaffa, lying on the horizon, backed by a hazy whiteness we knew for the sand-dunes that rose upon the shore.

The skies' immaculate blue touched them indistinctly, and that darker haze above them was the blue Mediterranean. Our thoughts flew homeward. The others turned away, and I and another captain stood alone. We were touched—as who could fail to be?—with the poetry of the scene. For a great view great thoughts. The camp, with its trivialities and round of tiresome detail, lay far below us, unseen and unheard. At our feet aromatic plants grew in abundance; scents that are familiar, but difficult to give a name to, escaped as we plucked and crushed them.

The distance we had come, the seas that separated us from home, the adventures that lay before us, the nature of the country, sacred and historic, we were shortly to tread, inspired us with a sense of kinship with events past and to come that broke down the narrow boundaries of personality and made us one with all the ages.

Moved by a natural impulse that came I knew not whence, I prayed in simple sentences for the victory of our division in the weeks to come. My mind flashed back to the high rock-perched church of Notre-Dame de Marseilles, where I had sent up an earlier prayer for the division on the eve of its departure from France. The officer who was with me then I had helped to bury not many days ago on a barren ridge south of the town of Beersheba.

We stayed at Latrun for a full week-end, receiving orders on Monday night to move the following morning. Everyone was refreshed, washed, cleaned up, renovated in body and soul and raiment, and there was no excuse that could detain us further. But we were loath to leave the place, in spite of its cold nights. We were going into still colder regions; the rains, of which our foretaste still lingered faintly in our memory, had not yet properly manifested themselves, though no one faced the fact. Just as we were packing up to move off, and while I was in the middle of the wicked act of burying a pile of maps of the country we had already passed,—maps of whose superfluous weight the battalion had refused to relieve me. Temple came up and said he wanted to see me.

"I'm awfully sorry, skipper," he said, "but it's no use. I can't go any further. You'll have to leave me behind. I've been having attacks of dysentery all the time we've been here, and I simply can't carry on any farther. That last march did for me. The worst of it is I always *look* all right. You'll have to take it on trust. I'm just going to report to the M.O."

I accepted his speech before he had come to the end of it, as I had accepted and survived many a calamity to the company during the past years. I was writing him off as he spoke, meeting the occasion, thinking which sergeant could best take his platoon. It would be an insult, I thought, to try to buck him up. I knew him for a sincere person. He had been with me for two years. He had done what he could.

"Right-ho! Temple," I said. "Beastly hard luck. Goodbye. Write to us when you get to Kantara. Hope you strike a good hospital. I say, look here: when you get better, don't forget to push some food up to the old company." Then, trying to be cheerful, I added: "Lucky dog, going back to civilization!"

"I'm awfully sorry," he reiterated, "but I'm afraid it's no good." And he went off mournfully to the M.O.

This sudden announcement left me in reality far from cheerful. The two officers who now remained to me were Jackson and Trobus. Jackson was nothing like so good at maps and compass work as Temple, though he was a very good disciplinarian, a much older man, and a strong fount of energy and devotion. Trobus, skittish young dog, might at any moment fall a victim once more to the lure and glory of being something connected with the division; I could never be sure now how long he was going to stay with me. If the worst happened, if Trobus disappeared and Jackson cracked up—he had begun latterly to talk about the way his bones ached and to hint rheumatism, and he looked perfectly awful when he woke up in the morning—I saw myself a lonely potentate, governing the savage tribe with the assistance of my burly sergeant-major.

These were the thoughts that passed through my mind as the Lewis gun teams clustered round the mules, stacking all kinds of weighty baggage on their backs—tin magazine boxes, long leather cases, the guns, protected by canvas covers, boxes of a different shape, carrying spare parts. At length all was ready, the ground well cleaned, everyone across the stream. Just as we were moving off, I noticed, to my astonishment, that Temple, though he was not carrying a pack, was back in his usual place with his platoon.

I rode up and called him aside.

"I thought you were on the way to Alex," (usual abbreviation for Alexandria), I said. "Are you all right again?"

"The doctor wouldn't let me go," said the poor boy, but he has excused my carrying a pack and has given me a pill. I expect it will kill me."

I could not help smiling, though I pitied him all the same. "Well, I'm jolly glad you've come back. I had written you off, you know. Try to stick it. Perhaps you'll be better tonight, and get to Jerusalem after all."

He shook his head. "I'm afraid not; I'm done in."

Lying in bed at Jerusalem, watching day by day a square of roof and three-quarters of a stone tower, which now would be traversed by a slow crawling shadow, now dimmed by storms that flecked the window, I often thought weeks later of the episode of Temple's return to the company at Latrun when by rights he ought to have gone down the line.

By rights, I say; but I do not blame the doctor. Would he have done it, though, if he had known what waited for the lad—the certainty of it? Temple was not strong, he was practically exhausted, he *ought* to have got away. Other officers had gone sick on grounds that were far slighter. It was just his "Joss." He had been cast for a slightly longer tour of duty, he could not turn off here. Other officers with half his pluck got leave home, and, for aught I know, are still bucking about. And I am still alive, writing about it. It passes my comprehension.

3: JERUSALEM WAY

The moon is shining through a tall French window in a little town near Lille. It falls upon a shell-smitten church in the square outside—poor place of worship, desolate now, with its cascade of stones tumbled to the street and its tall pile of rubbish. It shines upon me, only half-conscious, as I write, of these new scenes and surroundings. For still I bring forth thoughts that bear upon the past, and there is no rest for me until I have told my tale. The pictures in the back of my mind are not of a retreating German host, armistice-muzzled, shepherded and watched to their borders by us, the cavalry; I see instead a column of London troops, marching up a winding road, dusted white, and in a blaze of sun.

If you weary of adventures that hold such long tame periods in their compass, I can only tell you in a frank word that we, too, often wearied of them. But, if you too, like us on that bright morning, have any wish to know what sights lie round the bend, or love a tale for its own sake, although it be a quiet one, so that it remain true to life, plunge now with me into that past again. I promise young and old a right good piece of battling at the end of the story.

★★★★★★★★★★

We had not marched far before we realised that we were at the beginning of a long ascent. The road, passing at first through only slight acclivities of rocky slope or plough-land, became, as the advance continued, more and more shut in. A building of some kind on the right, and a track that led off and up and beyond it, marked the point where a gorge began. A slight curve to the left led us between two heights which rose almost sheer from the road, one with the sunlight shining on it, the other partially bathed in shadow. Since Macedonia we had not trodden mountain paths or known the joy of hills; it was exhilarating, in spite of the pull and the strain, to drink purer air and be winning towards heights which would give us wider horizons, and where we could cast great glances around and feel ourselves masters of more than a few miles of flat dirt.

The road was good; it had been improved some years before for the *Kaiser*, a fact that evoked laughter and some ironic witticisms— little had he thought that progress would indirectly benefit a column of his English enemies in the near years to come! From time to time an inhabitant of the country, Jew or Arab or nomadic *mélange* of both, would pass on shuffling slippers Latrun-wards, dusty, clad in nondescript-looking, sad-coloured robes girded up for travelling and showing thin brown legs, or jigging along on the backs of very small donkeys, toes just thrust into wide stirrups, legs jerking backwards and forwards in answer to the donkey's short quick paces. There was grandeur in the gorge as we plunged deeper into it, still ascending,

LONDON REGIMENT, JERUSALEM, 1917

between hills that showed no signs of petering out into table-lands, but rose ever higher, promising us greater heights beyond.

It was not long before we came to a building, established at the foot of the rocks, which almost overhung it—a building that was a cross between an inn, a toll-house, and the lair of a gang of robbers. It was an affair of two storeys, solidly built of great pieces of stone; but what most struck our fancy was a kind of open kitchen that adjoined it, which may have been a stable for post-horses, but looked like a shelter for wild fellows to meet together in at night and sit round a bonfire, brewing drinks, red wine of Palestine perhaps, or stronger liquids from the barley plains below, waiting for such as travelled Jerusalem-way without sufficient protection.

My bookish mind filled it with characters from the works of Borrow and Stanley Weyman, but not for long, for we did not pause here, and other features claimed our attention. The first halt, welcomed gladly enough, was in a little space where trees grew on the right of the road, backed by the rock's sheer wall. They were olives, showing, under a layer of white dust from the road, the dull metallic green of their small pointed leaves. In this delightful arbour of sun-chequered shade we snatched ten blissful minutes, time enough to enjoy a juicy Jaffa orange. We had not for many a long day rested in so shady a place, and the end of the ten minutes found us very loath to fall in again upon the road.

With the exception of a white house with trees round it, a well-built, pleasant-looking place, close to the road, nothing was passed during the next two or three miles, and still the road led upward. The usual grunts in chorus, an old stock joke when troops march uphill, had run down the ranks and been forgotten. This was the longest hill we had ever climbed, we thought, and here we were, still climbing it, and not a sign of the top.

After a while the cliffs on our left fell away and gave place to a great rocky ravine, dotted with olive-trees and showing occasional rude attempts at cultivation, where small plots of ground had been formed by carrying away the stones and piling them up into rough walls. But the most part was rocky waste, lying in half-defined terraces, until your eye sought the bottom and the dry bed of a torrent.

For some time we skirted this chasm, until at last rounding it, the road, now taking an easier gradient, made a great sweep to the left, and leaving the gorge behind, ran along a bare ridge, open at both sides to the slight mountain breeze. And now everyone exclaimed at the sight which lay to the left of them, for the height was such that we could look right over the hills through which we had ascended, and see the plain we had journeyed over on our way to Latrun, and, on the uttermost verge of it, catch the grey haze of the sea.

To the right the scene was scarcely less wonderful, for here were all manner of rocky formations, ravines that ran into each other, and misty tops of hills yet unapproached; a countryside of great barrenness, but not unlovely to the sight, for the prevailing colours were reds as of various English clays; and always the olive, stumpy, small and hardy and nourishing itself apparently on nothing, appeared at odd corners, to cheat us into believing that the land was fertile.

This turn in the road, and the steep approach to it, with a whole grove of trees on the right at the actual turn itself, formed a position of such natural strength that we all wondered how the approach had ever been forced. With a few machine-guns and a coil or two of barbed wire we were confident we could have held an army at bay; yet this was the road which, not so many days previously, had been conquered under cover of darkness and in storms of rain by the troops we were on the way to relieve.

To us, marching in the sunlight, the feat looked difficult enough, and we wondered at the dash and hardihood of their enterprise. Our contempt of the Turks grew as we considered this: they must have been poor fellows not to have made a better fight of it, and yet we knew them to be stubborn, and, however ill-nurtured, not prone easily to give up.

Here, for the third or fourth time, we rested, and the officers walked down the ranks and told the men that the midday halt was near. Some distance ahead, considerably higher than the rocks on which we lay, a white building that looked like a church but flew a Red Cross flag seemed to mark the highest point to which we should have to climb. Somewhere just short of this, the colonel had told me, the whole brigade would rest for at least two hours.

Then we were to continue the march, and go right into the line and relieve the Scots, who, we were told, were very battered and spent. For the Turk had sat down about Jerusalem in force, and had dug trenches, and, with enlisted German help and his own best battalions, was determined to pin us down to the hills until the rains should cut us from our transport and cause us and our beasts, the trains of far-brought camels, to die of exposure and want of food.

The troops we were relieving, and who had achieved so much,

had been arrested upon Nebi Samvil, and were unable to dislodge the enemy from the rocky ridges beyond. This was the task we were marching to tackle, though, as we rested on the hill-tops, we knew wondrously little about it. Nor had anyone any conception of what even the close of that day would bring. Sufficient unto the march the weariness thereof.

Another half-hour brought us to the spot chosen for the midday halt. Some hundred yards or so short of the white building that flew the Red Cross flag we turned off to the right, and scrambled for a short distance over the rocks, splitting up into companies as we did so. Before us lay a landscape typical of the more barren portions of Judaea, and difficult to bring before Western eyes. The companies, as they sat down, were grouped in bunches on the upper rocks of a great dip in the stony hills, in which there was not a blade of grass or a tree. Loose pieces of rock lay about all over it, but on the lower part the rocks were less frequent, and their place was taken by a dark and clayey earth covered with stony fragments.

It was difficult to walk anywhere, even in a soldier's heavy boots, but here and there you could trace what might have been paths used by goats, or shepherds, perhaps. Three parts of the way up the rocks began to range themselves more or less regularly in terraces, and amongst them were dark green growths of furzy nature, and some herbaceous plants. The hot sun beat down upon it all; the air was very clear, the detail stood out as in a stereoscopic view.

With the hills that sloped away on the far side, some stone-built houses visible on them in the far distance, the indistinct tops of other hills far beyond, the multitudinous terraces in their various tones of blue-grey, and the warm reds that everywhere put colour about them, it made a scene of open spaces whose very bareness and simplicity had in it something fresh and pleasant.

The men got out their beef and biscuits and dates, and we sat a little way apart, munching ours. For me it was all prologue to a ceremony I heartily wished was over. We were not the only battalion whose companies lay scattered about on the rocks, and this was the time chosen by the divisional general to make a presentation of any decorations that had been won at Sheria. It is impossible not to feel awkward and self-conscious when you know you have shortly to take part in an unusual piece of ceremonial.

At last, the moment for it grew near, and I slunk off in the direction of the road, where a red pennon marked brigade headquarters.

On the way I met two other officers, equally uncomfortable, and we all three stood there, talking about nothing, as nervous as if we were going to be married. After a few minutes small detachments of men marched up, a platoon of my own company and a platoon from the battalion to which one of the other officers belonged. Then followed more waiting and more foolish conversation. At last, the general arrived, and we stood in a row before all the men, stiffly at attention.

As we stepped forward in turn the general smiled and shook hands with us, and was very nice and said something different to each of us. I wondered if he could always think of something fresh to say. It was very tactful, and gave one the sense of being known as an individual, which is gratifying to poor human nature. Then the men were asked to give three cheers, and it was all over. I was sorry for the men, for whom this was not the first ceremonial parade of the kind, and I was particularly sorry to break the midday rest of my own. But it would be untruthful not to add that I went back very proud of my ribbon.

We lingered on for some time after this performance, and when at last we did move I was taken by surprise, and had to make the men put on their equipment quickly and hurry over the rocks back on to the road. It was, I remember, the middle of the afternoon when the march thus recommenced, and I believe it was about now that I learnt we were marching to bring off a relief.

Latrun seemed far away, our pleasant interlude there an affair of the distant past; the unknown, too, appealed to our fancy, and led us on, for we were fresh and not incurious of adventures to come. There was always a chance of getting a glimpse of Jerusalem somehow, the men thought, and the idea of a possible sight of it was vaguely present also in the minds of some of our officers.

Then we were going again into a battle-zone, after a long period of marching, nearing some sort of a line; would be, in fact, that night once more in presence of the enemy. This was stimulating, and exciting and new. I have never discovered exactly how my men feel in these matters: perhaps the spirit of adventure does not dwell in their hearts, but I know they love to talk about what they have done, about scenes and experiences like these, when they are over.

But I love the pageant of it, and manage to extract pleasure even out of the most dismal situations, if they have any touch of romance about them. And was this not romantic, to be marching like the Romans to Jerusalem, and nearly to be at the point where marches would end and the expected struggle begin? Did the men of the legions of

Titus grouse at the bad going as they tramped up into Judaea? How different to them Jerusalem, only the troublesome and insubordinate city of a pestilential people!

We topped the hill, passed the white flag-crowned hospital on our left, caught a sight of the stone walls of a monastery, and so were away, treading a downward road, with En Nab behind us. I knew that our route did not lie much longer on the highroad, but that a track that was marked on the map "Roman Road" led off on the left into country at whose nature we could hardly guess. The turning came sooner than we had expected, at a place where a number of ambulance waggons stood among some trees, a resting-place that at some periods of the year must have been pleasant and fertile. But now, when everything longed for the rains, it was parched and dusty-dry.

The "Roman Road" must have deteriorated considerably since the time the legions trod it, for it was but a track differing only from the country on either side by being clear of loose rocks. Past the plantation we began to climb up again, and soon were in the midst of a wilderness of volcanic rock. The scene was wild in the extreme. To our left a great valley or *wadi* stretched far below in a chaos of majestic disorder; at its lowest point the dry bed of a water-course lay contorted; on the remotest slopes a few olive-trees eked out their gnarled lives. There was dusty soil on the upland ridge where we were treading, and on the right the ground rose gradually to the rounded summit of the hill whose upper slopes we trod.

Presently we came upon a noticeboard, stuck up among some loose rocks on the right, a warning to troops to beware of enemy fire—out-of-date, perhaps, but sufficient to remind us that business was afoot. Shortly after this we passed the ruins of a wide pit, or well. Then the "Roman Road" became invisible or we left it, for we found ourselves picking our way in file along a goat-track.

This was the beginning of trouble. Up to this point little strain had been experienced by the men, beyond the fatigue of a well-managed march. The strange new scenery against which they had been moving had not unpleasantly diverted their attention from themselves.

But now everything came upon us at once to defeat and to discourage. A path that to a civilian traveller loaded only with light haversack seems curiously rugged, nothing more, may tax all the powers of endurance of a man so loaded that heavy weights seem hanging on his feet. The strain on a fully equipped infantryman is tremendous if he has not a fairly free passage to tread; it requires great individual

INFANTRY OF THE 60TH DIVISION AT REST

determination for him to bear up under such dead weight hour after hour. The morning's long ascent from Latrun, despite the mid-day rest, had taken something of every man's stock of energy. No one knew exactly where the "line" was, or how long a tramp we had before us, and thus not one of us could brace himself to accomplish a definite task. The track was not so very bad; in Macedonia we had navigated pathways ten times worse; but never since Beersheba had anything so hard and uncompromising presented itself.

The path followed many petty turns as various as a piece of string takes, carelessly thrown down upon the ground. Into it and over it at every angle slabs and fragments of rock jutted or lay atilt. As the old weariness descended on the plodding files, everyone became an individual again and began, silently and resolutely, to tackle his own share of the problem. Non-commissioned officers were just men, so many more plodding individuals, bent on accomplishing a task. They were all "sticking it," each in his own way, for personal reasons never properly thought out, but related to something larger than a company or a battalion. They were, in fact, for good or ill, not professional soldiers but civilians, self-enrolled to get a job done. A very difficult crowd to deal with, but one at whose feet many great personages would do well occasionally to sit.

Luckily for us, the light held during this part of the march, or we should have suffered very great troubles and delays. After what seemed a long space of time, though it may not have been more than two hours, we arrived at some buildings and saw some of the Scots transport, near a stone wall. Here our own transport left us: it seemed we were getting fairly near to our goal. Presently we moved off again. In a few minutes the light had gone, and we were marching under a pale moon.

I do not remember clearly what happened during the next half-hour, but I know that it was either near the stone wall, or shortly after we left it behind us, that one of the Scots joined himself on to my company and said that he was a guide. Thus much, I understood, but the rest of his conversation was almost unintelligible. Led by him, we now passed over an area where the face of the rock lay flat in great pavements, very slippery to walk over. These tabular formations, we found afterwards, are not uncommon, and it is upon such natural foundations that stone houses are built.

Now I realised for the first time the absolute propriety and vivid appeal of the parable of the builder—a parable that in England I had always considered rather exaggerated and strained. The apparently firm ground down in the valley turns quickly to mud in the violent winter rains, and in many places becomes the bed of a watercourse, but these rocky sites defy all weathers. A little further on several shadowy stone walls appeared; then we passed between some flat-roofed buildings, all of stone, in a place where there was nothing anywhere but stone, and even the wood of a narrow door looked precious.

After this, I know not how, the ground became more open, and we found ourselves tumbling on loose stones of a smaller kind, and knew that we were descending into a wide space of comparatively low-lying ground, down a kind of valley or hollow between two hills. The company seemed to be coming along better now that it had left behind it those monotonous stretches of high mountain track; the presence of the guide told all of us that we were on the last stage; the path we were now treading was easier, in spite of the stones and the uncertain light; we had dropped a few stragglers, it is true, but all knew the worst was over.

During our descent the valley opened out until we were dimly aware that we had come into a great space. A few minutes past we had seen on our right the horrid bodies of dead camels, mounds of flesh, a revolting sight to look at in the moonlight. The beasts, our guide told me, had been shelled as they came into view, some days ago. Now that we were on the flat (say, rather, the *comparatively* flat, for nothing is flat in Judaea), I compressed the company into column of fours again, in order to have it more handy. While I was waiting in this dark and silent valley for the rearward weaklings to come up, I tried to get some elementary information out of my Scots guide touching the position his company (which I was about to relieve) was holding, and how they were holding it.

He was willing enough to tell, but his mouth was so full of dialect that I boggled over every explanation he offered. Politeness and shame at being so slow to catch the gist had made me at length pretend I understood, so by this time I had drifted into a hopeless conversational slough, the way into it paved by about fifteen successive misunderstandings. All I could gather was that he was "fed up," and that he was taking us to an awful place—a place that he would be glad to get out of, a fact he stated over and over again, in his own language, with many varieties of interjection and emphasis.

He bore so battle-worn an air, was so full of obscurely expressed hints of impossibilities achieved, but not to be achieved again if he

A TYPICAL VILLAGE

could help it; had so obviously been "in it" and "through it," and now so obviously wanted to be "out of it," was withal so openly aware that we had escaped this particular bit of it—that I felt almost like a new boy beside him—a fellow who so far had been nowhere and done nothing.

At last, the company was "all up." The message came to me like a breath of thankfulness, after being whispered high and low by twenty successive voices. Even the Lewis-gun mules, watched over and shepherded by Jackson, herdsman in general of the rear, stood in full tally in the moonlight, lumps of unutterable woe. Now we began to move on again, wheeling slightly to the left as we crossed the vale, nervously trusting the guide would pilot us safely to a certain low rocky hill, at present nothing but a mass of blackness with a broken ridge to it. This I judged was to be our position.

As we came nearer low walls appeared, made of loose piled pieces of flat rock, the old boundaries of two or three stony fields. A few skilful turns and twists on the part of the Scot, and we were standing at the base of an irregular series of low heaps of volcanic rock, on the other side of which stood outposts, mute representatives of the furthest limits of British power in Palestine. Four guides came out of the shadows as we approached and attached themselves each to a platoon.

In spite of the moon, the position of which I forget, the night was dark, and it was only just possible to make out the place immediately before us. To get the hang of it straight away was a task beyond anyone's powers. What we saw were the edges or shadowy indications of a number of ledges or terraces, piled one upon another, with every variety of fault and twist in them, themselves only bits of accidental uniformity that ran amok amidst the heaped waste and general confusion of the place. The job was to get the relief over as quickly as possible. Nothing could be done, however, until the Lewis guns had been taken off the mules, for two of them at least were wanted in the outpost line.

These are the apparently simple matters that require all the energy, common sense, resourcefulness, authority, and good-humour officers are expected to possess. The tale of their performance fills up the greater part of the history of war treated as human experience. The difficulties on this occasion were diverse. Firstly, the men were so exhausted that it was not easy to get them to obey any order intelligently and quickly. Secondly, all orders had to be given in sepulchral whispers. The cramped and awkward lie of the ground made a third difficulty; the darkness a fourth. Yet this act was but one particular trouble in a night that could be counted on—experience had taught us—to provide a rich crop of them.

It was impossible to unload the mules where we stood, for we were right in the road of the company that would shortly be going away. Nor was it easy to choose a place for this operation. It soon became evident that this rocky hill was densely inhabited by men who were squatting, ready to move, on almost every flat ledge it afforded. I also quickly discovered that a battery of light guns had taken permanent possession of the place, and that the guns themselves were in position in the very middle of the infantry. I tried to find the headquarters of the company I was relieving, but was told, in a flood of Scots, that there wasn't a headquarters and that the captain was in the line.

But some good resulted from this first quick inspection, for I found, somewhat to the right of where most of the men were waiting, a stony ledge wide enough to take eight men abreast, and long enough, apparently, to enable a company to be pushed along it and leave a clear space for the mules to be unloaded in the rear. A place where two lower ledges had collapsed within a few yards of each other made it possible for the company to be got up by the execution of a snake-like movement, and by dint of much scrambling, some straggling, and several patience-exasperating checks. The mules, pair by pair, came scrambling up by a kind of desperate last effort.

While I was watching the mules, and showing their leaders where I wanted them, the platoons tramped grimly and stolidly on round the corner, and had to be turned about and shepherded back again. This mistake made no impression on the men, who now were so tired that they had become automata. Next it was necessary to get the four Lewis-gun teams to come and find their mules and get their stuff off. This took an incredible time, and during it the company sat down and went to sleep.

At last, the miserable gunners were driven back to their platoons, the numerous leather valises and tin cash-boxes that Lewis-gunners find it necessary to haul painfully about with them were stacked in a solid square heap, mule-leaders and their beasts were told to clear right off (No, I didn't know where they were to go to), and the company was kicked up to face the job again.

Three platoons were to be in the line, and one in reserve, but as the fourth, it appeared, occupied a vaguely specified position midway between the line and where I was standing, or else half-way round the hill, to the right (the guide said it could not be explained, but he knew), all four were despatched immediately, and I was left with my headquarters, which, in spite of constant cutting down and strict supervision, was nearly as big as a platoon. For the moment nothing could be done but wait the arrival of runners, bringing the news that the platoons had "taken over."

I determined to stay where I was. It was not a bit of use going to look for the Scots company commander: we might chase each other round the rocks all night. At this moment Seattle came up: "I've got your valise, sir; where would you like your bivouac?"

Preoccupied with the chief matter, the management of the relief, this sudden intrusion of my domestic arrangements seemed nothing but a bother. There was something comic, too, in the detachment of Seattle from the greater business, his entire absorption in my petty affairs. My vision, which ranged over the whole valley in speculative flight and had already constructed out of the general murkiness the probable sort of landscape that existed on the other side of the ridge, where the relief was taking place, now had to come home for a moment and look after a practical detail. "O anywhere," I said, and then repented instantly of the rash word, and began to cast swift glances at the jumbled masses of rocks about me.

Towards the base of our ridge a last terrace seemed fairly clear of stone, and the moonlight fell upon a small portion of it that looked as if it was covered with earth. "There you are, Beattie," I said; "that's the place. Do what you can. I'll come and help later."

Inactivity in the midst of activity adds untold weariness to strained and anxious minds. I had set aside a very liberal margin of time for the platoons to accomplish their task, and still no one reported, no one came. At last, after a period of tedium civilian life never knows, one of those cold vacua in which long minutes lapse and pass while the cow-like mind wallows in sounds and colours of the bygone day, a string of shadowy figures appeared among the rocks, and I knew that one of the Scots platoons had been relieved. A few words with its commander, and it passed on.

Presently one of my runners arrived. He had lost his way. From him I learnt what was happening on the other side of the hill. Slowly, painfully, with many small "mess-ups," the relief was coming through its customary throes. Last of all, long after I had supposed him gone, the Scots company commander appeared, with his band of followers. He was very surprised that I had not been looking for him. I did not attempt useless explanations. He was almost as difficult to understand as his lowland slave—the trusty guide he had sent me.

I wished him luck and secretly prayed he would call his remaining people about him and leave this part of Judaea. One always feels like that about departing company commanders. At length the last Scot picked up the last pack, and the confused landscape was wholly left to us and to the battery.

Choosing the most trustworthy of my runners, I now set forth to visit the line, to do my duty and to satisfy my curiosity as to what existed on the other side of the ridge. The best way of getting there was to work round the right shoulder of it, where it declined, by an irregular series of semi-circular terraces, into the valley. Two-thirds of the way round and almost at its base a row of low cairns backed close against the solid stone of a terrace afforded some shelter for the reserve platoon. We found these habitations after much wandering, for there was no path to them and the formation of the rocks was so eccentric that no bearings could be taken by the eye.

To follow the inviting road of a terrace was to be taken insidiously into the valley or to the top of the hill, or gradually to a beach of rocks with a slice of unclimbable sheer rock above and an awkward drop below. The platoon was in position, but had a very hazy idea as to where the line was. I therefore took one of the men with me, so that someone at least would know the way in case of emergency.

Further silent wandering of about a quarter of an hour brought us to the other side of the ridge. We were three-quarter way down the upper portion of a long slope of stones that passed into an open valley which finally, at a distance of about a mile, rose by very pronounced terraces of rock into another ridge. But the distances appeared greater than they really were, and our hill very high and black at the back of us. We seemed to be standing in a wilderness of stones.

To our right the valley at the back of the ridge we were defending curved forward, and spreading out into a great hollow, became one with the open country in front. On the further side of the vale, how far off we could not tell, a hill, in comparison with which our lodgement was only a tumbled heap of rock, stood like a dark sentinel, a small light just visible on its forward slope. This was the terminating point of another ridge that helped to shut in the valley behind us, and its name was Nebi Samvil.

Description of very irregular country is nearly as painful as walking over it, and photographs are not much better than words. I should like to see a painting of Judea by moonlight in the neighbourhood of

Nebi Samvil. I thought that night how rough a place it was. We found later worse places awaited us.

This new scenery we took in at a few glances: it was not so easy to discern the position of the outposts. The gradual slope in front of us, the masses of piled rocks behind, seemed equally uninhabited. I was thinking of proceeding further, when one of the runners said he thought he had seen something moving, behind us and to the left. Turning round, and looking very carefully, I saw enough to convince me that we were a good distance in front of our own outposts.

Walking very quietly, and making to the right, I got back out of this dangerous position as quickly as I dared, my heart beating loudly enough to remind me that I was very much alive. Even if I had been seen, I did not think my men would shoot without a challenge, but there was the possibility.

Shortly after this little adventure I came upon the men themselves, the right post of my part of the line. The first question I asked was if they had seen anything in front of them. They answered "No." I felt so small at having lost the way that I hadn't the face to "tick them off" for not seeing me, but inquired instead the position of the next post. One of them pointed the direction, and I set off again.

Incredible as it may seem, in four minutes I had again lost the way, and after some wandering found myself in front of post number two. This time I met a challenge. At length I found the end of my complicated piece of front.

The difficulty lay chiefly in the way the Scots had defended the position. They had piled up stone *sangars* on the face of the hill at varying heights and in places where there was sufficient earth to make excavations. The result was a very irregular series of detached posts, extremely difficult to follow out by night. By day, it seemed, we should never see them until the military situation changed, for the line was held by an observation post only, consisting of one Lewis-gun team, who relieved the night team just before morning twilight.

Satisfied at last that all was reasonably correct, I went back to find the colonel. I discovered him in his valise-bivouac, bed and tent combined, which he had erected up against a rock, not far from my small plateau but lower down, and closer to the lee of the hill. He was glad to hear the line was in position, told me I was an ass to bivouac on the ledge I had chosen, that I should probably be shelled next morning and that the "overs" would hit him. Then he ceased speaking and slept.

The good Beattie had put up my small tent. My valise was invitingly laid out inside—the old brown bundle that carried all my possessions. My shaving tackle was disposed on a folded ground-sheet beside it: Beattie had really done very well. It is wonderful how happy man can be with few possessions, given a good job and a good master. The night was far advanced. I crawled in. It was a splendid bed: all the little bits of rock had carefully been removed from the site before the bivouac had been pitched. These were the only things that troubled my last thoughts in the darkness.

I think it had been the longest, fullest day I had ever lived through—longer even than a day of early childhood. We had started from Latrun and now we had taken over the line. So far, the enemy had not disturbed us: one might easily imagine he was not there at all. Tomorrow something might happen. But tomorrow could take care of itself.

CHAPTER 4

On the Heights

1: SEDENTARY WARFARE

The period we spent at this queer portion of the line was not very strenuous as outpost positions go, and not over-dangerous, and yet it was arduous enough and full of anxiety, despite occasional hours of happiness and quiet. We were hard up for men, and the nightly duties came too often to allow the company any real repose. Every dodge had been tried; every subaltern had come forward in turn with schemes of "washing out" some of the posts or reducing the number of men on existing ones; yet from these experiments no permanent relief had resulted. The nights were extremely cold; the watching strained men's nerves to the uttermost.

Our defences were of the flimsiest—a few holes in the ground protected by rough stone barricades. The ground was open in front of the sentry-line, it is true, but Turks are very clever at crawling up to a position, and most of our reliance was placed on the continuance of clear, moonlit nights. Moreover, we lived in a battery-position, right amongst the guns, a place well worth the taking. Though I, personally, was not very nervous about all this, mainly because I was feeling extremely well and partly because I had great confidence in my officers and men, the colonel, whose responsibility is greater, was obviously not a little solicitous; the second-in-command, too, our impetuous major, spent not a little time testing the various groups.

The old game I knew so well started soon after daybreak the first day after our arrival. Small shells came rushing overhead, landing, most of them, in the flattish ground behind us that stretched from the base of our hill. We were forced to cling very close and lead an ant-like existence. There was a small tree on the forward slope of Nebi Samvil, and the Scots had left a caution with us that when you had walked round the right shoulder of our hill and could see the whole of the tree you were in danger. Needless to say, no one was allowed to put his head over the top, and so, though we were living on a perfectly open piece of country, we were in reality as constrained as if we were in trenches.

To these dangers and limitations, you must add, properly to visualise the scene, the precautions necessary with regard to our own guns. The battery was the most enterprising and the most dangerous I have ever lived with. Placed right amongst the men's small tents, they fired away, first in one direction and then in another, as if we were not there. Our Londoners, who had long grown accustomed to risk, were so careless that the gunners had constantly to keep shouting to them to get their heads out of the light. The guns were a new type, twelve- or fourteen-pounders, I believe, and they made a great noise, and jumped about when they were fired.

My subalterns, Jackson, Temple, and Trobus, were living happily and peaceably together at this period, and had clubbed sheets and made a long shelter, open at the front, backed up against the solid rock. To this they obstinately clung, though a noisy gun about four yards away shook it every time it fired and filled it with smoke. I, on my supposedly dangerous ledge, was far better off. The Scots had left a number of biscuit-tins behind them, and very early in the morning Beattie and I collected a few. Filled with stones, they made a splendid wall to block up the gable-end of my tent, and with three of the remaining ones I made the best stove I have ever constructed.

One thing contributed to the happiness of everyone, the fact that the battery became a universal provider of wood for our fires. The wood supply, now and for weeks past, had always been in the forefront of our thoughts, and "our daily wood" was as natural a thing to pray for as our bread. These energetic and hard-working gunners were very generous in giving away their shell-boxes, and we came to rely on them for fuel to such an extent, and were so unusually well off, that I remember thinking of the place, days afterwards, as "the position in which there was wood."

"Sedentary warfare," an expression first introduced to us on the Vardar by our brigadier-general, who loathed it with a peculiar hate, is not unpleasant to me. Some of the happiest, as well as the most miserable, days of my life have been spent at "positions," in France, in Macedonia, and here at Nebi Samvil. There is the schoolboy sense of fun and importance at having a definite place to hold; shells, if they do not exceed a certain number per hour, merely give a pleasurable sense of excitement to what otherwise would be rather a humdrum life, and there is generally plenty of constructive work to be done, in which I take great joy.

The broken tales let fall from the lips of the Scots had screwed us up for anything, and we should not have been surprised to have been attacked by a host of crawling Turks on the evening of our first day: more than one of our clerkly soldiers had no doubt imagined them coming up with knives between their teeth, as he stood watching the rocks in the moonlight, shivering with cold at his post. Yet, by an odd chance, it fell out that we inherited a batch of peaceful days, though without doubt the Scots had fared differently behind this barren ridge.

There was a second battery hidden on some slightly rising ground in the valley just behind us, and these guns attracted a good deal of the enemy fire. And so, it fell out that, though we were the unwilling guests at an artillery duel of some persistence, we got off with nothing but close shavers: I do not remember a single casualty. This immunity did not extend to other parts of the line. A runner proceeding westwards towards Nebi Samvil itself would find himself, as he began to climb the hill, in a very hot place. Shells were always bursting over the remains of the old *mosque*, whose minaret, once a landmark for miles, had been knocked to pieces a few days before our arrival.

The Turks hated us to be in possession of this dominating spot, and day after day battle raged fiercely about it. Violent attacks were made: some were nearly successful, and after a day or two the battalion defending it had to be withdrawn, and one from our own brigade went up to take its place. Our share in the fighting consisted of a solitary patrol action, an unfortunate business in which one of our men was killed; nor could we recover his body.

There was something about this period of calm which boded trouble to come. Anxious for news, asking for it from chance-arrivals, stray runners perhaps, or wanderers from other units, we never got anything to hold our thoughts. Troops were still coming up, preliminary dispositions for a great attack were being made; clearly the final assault upon the defences of Jerusalem was at hand, but when and where the main blow would be delivered no one knew. Indeterminate local actions held us, in this transitory stage, pinned to our ridge of rock, the sweep of the valley behind us.

The picture remains in clear detail. The heaps of stony rocks behind which we and the battery squatted were almost entirely destitute of vegetation, but the backward view appeared to my eye beautiful indeed. Across the dip a gradually rising slope, where earth lay in greater quantities than rock, bore on its upper portions, groups of old olive-trees, at whose feet was the pleasant shimmer of grass.

Lower down the hillside the soil was rich and plentiful, deep black in the rock-clefts and dark *terra-cotta* in the dip. This slope, the loveliest part of the valley, was nearest to us as you crossed the dip, but it was only a forward feature of a general ridge that wandered on until it ended bluntly in Nebi Samvil. The slope's other shoulder shrugged back into an amphitheatre of natural terraces improved into dry built walls, boundaries to little plots of tilled ground set at different levels.

Higher up came walls of a more substantial kind, and then a house or two, low, flat-roofed, stone-white, the outlying buildings of a village. Slightly to the right the village itself was partly visible, a few olive-trees about it, a small place, ancient and solid as the hills themselves. Here, arching over our heads in deliberate flight, shells burst, playing sad havoc amongst the unfortunate peasants, who would not leave their homes. Olive-green and clay-red were the prevailing tints, very dark and rich in the light of the early morning sun, which showed a landscape that was lustrous indeed, bathed and rejuvenated in the night's deep dews. By noon you had a different land, dry, parched and pale, a place to toil hard on to get a living, bringing to your lips the phrase "burden and heat of the day."

Afternoon shepherded the countryside to the sweet beauties of old age—delicate colours, a little faded, russets, browns and greys. Then perhaps would come one of those curious interregna of the East when sun and moon disputed equal rights, a period of Coleridgean charm. And while you gazed you shivered, for suddenly the sun was gone, and the valley had opened out beneath the moonshine, and the rocks had multitudes of blacker shadows born to them, so palpable that you almost felt that you could stroke them, like the backs of black cats.

In such surroundings, conscious that everything lay hidden in the lap of the next three weeks, not knowing that the sands had almost run out, we laboured to learn our position thoroughly, and waited what might befall. In the company everything was going well, but I continued the custom I had begun about the time this story opens, and took my meals by myself, being cooked for by my servant, with whom I shared equally such extra food as came my way.

A tin of Quaker Oats, which suddenly arrived in a parcel all the long way from Alexandria, made an extraordinary difference to my life; indeed, I am ashamed now to say how rosy everything looked after its arrival. I made lovely platefuls of the porridge and took them up to the subalterns, who were radiant with gratitude and pleasure. Battalion headquarters, who had formed a dining-room table in the open, just below me, made entirely out of old biscuit-tins, did not do nearly as well as Seattle and I, though their dates and biscuits and slices of bully were served in greater state.

I was revelling in a patent stove made out of yet more of the ubiquitous tins, a wonderful producer of heat and conserver of fuel and belcher of smoke. The fumes and smother of my cooking blew generally into the battalion mess, and a slight clash of interests arose. No shells arrived on my ledge, and I cooked and slept with impunity, thriving mightily. On the second or third day the major, always keen on nosing around in search of things normally unprocurable, announced that he had got some red wine, and would we like some. Assuredly. Then would we bring our mugs, mess-tins, pots, or cans? Sufficient were not available, and we fell as a last resource into filling up numbers of tin canisters that had held charges for the guns.

Out of one of these strange drinking-cups we tasted for the first time the heavy, sweet red wine of Palestine, and found it much to our taste. We did not drink to the success of our enterprise, for we had made part of it so long that it was only at times it came into our minds at all.

It was impossible to see very much of the men, for, though we were very much hunched up together on our barren slag-heap, we had to lie concealed and to avoid the slightest movement, and the chaos of rocks divided us into very small separate parties. But at night, in going round the line, or spending part of it on duty, I had many long conversations with the runners I took with me and with the sentinels I visited. Together we would stand in the moonlight, in the biting cold of those high regions, and I would hear about the job at home left on a burning impulse, and so much hankered after now, have talk about places we both knew, our speech broken into momentarily by questions as to whether a certain black spot on the moonlit slope were human or not, and resumed when the tension was relaxed.

One had to take care, stumping about amongst the boulders by night, for not a few pits had been quarried of old on the ridge, for storing either grain or water, and very often they were only carelessly covered over by a few slabs of loose rock. One night, looking for a place to sleep in, somewhere midway between the bivouac and the line, I came upon my very ideal conception of a rock-tomb—a long slit about four feet high cut in the face of a big rock. In it, prone on my valise, I spent the night, and a very hard couch it made.

Lying there, one of those strange moods came upon me in which the soul is deeply conscious of existence, and I thought over every detail of the Bible-story where it speaks of the new tomb, the preparations, the loving-care; and then criticism jumped up—the tendency to treat it as a myth, or a tale that doesn't matter. Then all the old life of Palestine came back and was real to me, and Europe seemed a strange foreign mistress who had only *coquetted* with a drama that belonged to the East.

The old problems went chasing through my brain—the precise significance of our presence here, what *we* were doing, blowing shells about this ancient bit of the world to help an indirect settlement of our Western quarrel, rather unimportant, perhaps, in comparison with *that*. Or was all action and contest nothing but a neutral background formed to give endless opportunities for exhibitions of the morale of man? The adjustment of a candle in a biscuit-tin insufficiently shaded broke off the speculation as easily as it had begun, and my flibberty-gibbet spirit turned, on the arrival of the sergeant-major, to matters of immediate policy. There was just room for us both—for him, the great broad-shouldered, blue-eyed fellow I had come to rely on, and for myself.

I was something luxurious that night, for I had made an arrangement with Beattie to squander in a pot of water my last Lazenby soup-square—an act of sufficient importance for a person at that time and in those parts to warrant it being set down in fair black and white. For it is these little suppers in rock-tombs and chance talks by the way, and odd hourly adventures of no historical weight, that yet make up the fabric of every man's experience.

Half an hour earlier I had written home from the tomb, and now the sergeant-major was here, and it wanted not long before the arrival of Beattie with biscuits and a covered pot—the fruits of Mr. Lazenby's genius (mulligatawny) all duly dissolved.

Uncomfortably, but with the naive pleasure of schoolboys, we supped together, and I read aloud to the head of my N.C.O. world a vivid tale of Stacpoole's about a fugitive thief who was caught and eaten by a giant squid on a coral reef in the Pacific. How we enjoyed it! The human soul is never sated with adventure.

About this time our divisional general (who was subject to sudden inspirations) decreed that a certain number of very deserving subalterns (I forget how the document was worded) should, instead of getting such barren rewards as the Military Cross or the D.S.O., be given a week's leave to go where they liked, providing they didn't walk into the enemy's lines. In our battalion the lot fell upon Temple, who certainly deserved this much appreciated favour.

I forget where the seven days was to begin to count from—railhead, I believe—but Temple, after much discussion in the smoke-filled bivouac (the restless gun belching at intervals over our heads and making us able at intervals to feel the very tips of our toes) decided not to go all the way to Cairo or Alexandria, but have a longer time at Port Said, which, though horrid enough, is not nearly so detestable a place as it appears to have been in the old days.

Directly it became known that he was going, deputations began to arrive, imploring him to buy everything in the small domestic line modern man desires—soap, looking-glasses, tooth-brushes, razors, scissors, pencils, pads of writing-paper. Filled with a kind of new dispensing power, he dealt with everyone according to his whim, but my own orders were a dead cert, for was I not his company commander? I remember him walking off, a figure envied even by battalion headquarters, with his valise balanced on a mule he had somehow wrung out of Hoyle, the transport officer, who now led an obscure existence somewhere behind the village in rear of us, supposed the traditional Emmaus.

He will come back again in the third division of this chapter, after a night of adventure on our part I am glad he was lucky enough to miss. It is vain to wish he had turned his week into a fortnight, for no one can dodge his destiny. Still, I am very glad to think he had that week. On the same day, or very soon afterwards, Trobus the irrepressible disappeared on a new job—something in the minor way on the divisional staff. I was sorry to lose him, particularly at this juncture, for it meant hard work and worry, as Jackson and I had to run the company alone.

Hardly had Trobus left us, when it was rumoured round we were in for another move. Someone went on behalf of my company to explore the route, a very necessary mission. I am sure it was not Jackson. Some subaltern must have been lent to me at this point, but my memory absolutely fails to picture him. I can see the mules stumbling up the dark terraces, and someone is leading the way. I follow, trying to have faith in him. Who was that shadowy person?

2: CHANGE OF POSITION

Battles are not easily joined in modern war: the marshalling of the troops takes time: long and painstaking adjustment of the pawns is necessary before the game is set. Complicated reliefs, much tramping to and fro, precede the delivering of a blow. Battalions perform enormous step dances with each other; headquarters of brigades rear their red pennons on unaccustomed rocks: there are dislocations, periods of suspense, of isolation. Even in quiet moments, when nothing is toward, there is always a certain amount of creeping movement in the army that has installed itself by pieces among these hills. Slow files of men with their attendant trains of mules and camels are to be seen in the moonlight, taking up a position or moving out of it at any hour of these fateful nights.

Within the battalions, platoons play with each other the same weary game on a tiny scale. Should movement cease, a slumber as of death would creep irresistibly upon the host. It would become immobile, prey to a thousand diseases. Power to manoeuvre would depart from it. Initiative, potent talisman, would pass one night to the enemy. This is the doctrine of our armies, which, except a general believe faithfully, he will be bowler-hatted.

To a nation of colonists, to a people who have the building instinct and who start making homes for themselves directly they are let alone, even if only for a day, this nomad life is one of constant disappointment. Soldiers ought not to expect to settle down, but time after time these domestic tendencies blinded us to the laws that governed our new life, and led us to embark on schemes doomed at the outset to pitiful non-completion. The general commanding our brigade, who had never felt an impulse to build a hut for himself, but who travelled (secretly, let it be said) in true Eastern manner with a carpet, sniffed at our ant-like industry, and called us more than once a set of gipsies.

It is probable that the gipsy leads a happier life than the soldier, though not so respectable a one. The difference for us lay between the amateur and the professional. Nothing on earth, not even the stains of many battles, could turn our clerks into members of a regular army. They were all descendants of John Gilpin, and he was a citizen in the first line of his poem and a trained-band captain only in the third. Generally, they could be relied on to salute with sufficient frequency to satisfy the demigods, but that sort of thing was frankly recognised as part of a mysterious game, supposed, in some dark, indirect way, to help on the war. Now, led up on to these tumbled highlands, clinging to their sheets—the pieces of roof that covered them at night—they made forlorn figures, these inhabitants of a great modern town going without any of the props they used to rely on.

No man can wander in Judaea's wildernesses and remain a smug person: how could they any longer answer to the narrow phrase "the man in the street"? Many wonders that the world held, but which had not existed for them, were now being forced upon their notice. There was, for example, moonlight on mountain-tops. The change was not apparent in their conversations, but various deep-seated revolutions had taken place within. Their experiences will find tongue in later generations; whereby our literature will be enriched.

Once again, the old fiat went forth, and we prepared to hand over our inhospitable ridge. Rumour had become fact: we were to visit a fresh position somewhere beyond the hill in our rear. Late in the afternoon a small advance party arrived, couriers of the troops to come. Everything went on as usual up to the last moment. Nothing could happen until darkness fell. In December, in this part of the world, the days close in rapidly, and half-past five is the beginning of night. The camels were to go by a route of their own, all together, I learnt after a short conversation with the adjutant. I found him in his small bivouac lying with his old master the telephone.

Squatting at the door, I listened to his plans, nodding when I thought them good and expressing strong opinions when I did not. I wanted to take my camels as well as my mules, for one of them carried my valise and Jackson's, slung in a rope net, and I did not want to lose sight of them. My old official enemy assured me, however, almost in pleading tones, that his arrangements were very good, and I had to give in.

"You'd never get the camels up those terraces," he said.

I looked, and saw that the argument was cogent. "As long as the beasts turn up at the end . . ."

"You can rely on that. Anything else? Goodbye."

We plundered those gunners as a last farewell to them, and I don't know how many shell-boxes the men of my company managed to smash up and carry on their backs in the form of kindling. At the foot of the ridge, three shadowy platoons stole up one after the other, and squatted near a jumbled collection of animals—my much-enduring mules. Here, with my court of followers, I waited for the last platoon to emerge from the line. It was a dark night, and great trouble had been taken to prevent confusion. After waiting nearly twenty minutes, I went to each of the three platoons, and discovered, on the other side of the mules, the missing one, fast falling asleep.

It had never crossed the mind of the sergeant to report that he had arrived. Each company had had separate orders; we were entirely on our own: all we had to do was to get to the next position. It was, I had been told, a place in reserve, where there would be no sentry-duty, and the men were cheerful in consequence, for they expected a holiday. We peeled off in a long, snake-like column, the mules in rear, bound over to the stern care of Jackson.

I was in front, on foot, and in front of me again, hopping about with some sworn ally of a runner, was the officer who had smelt out the way, the shadowy personage who has faded from my memory. We went, as usual, at the pace of a walking funeral. Our guide's first anxiety was to get to a certain tree. Everything depended, he said, on whether he could rediscover it.

As the slope was dotted with olives all of which looked exactly the same, I was not happy about his chances, but we hit it by a fluke, followed a little path for a short distance, and then bent left to tackle the terraces. Could the mules do it? Oh yes, there was a way. Had he not made holes in the walls that very afternoon? We vanquished the first terrace at the extreme left-hand corner, after feeling along it for about fifty yards.

Ten yards further on we were face to face with another. This we breached half-way up, as the hole he had previously made could not be found. The next two terraces were ruinous; we scrambled up and over them fairly easily. Then came a blank piece of rock. Happily, the moon was rising, but its light only showed more terraces above us, and one or two stone buildings at the top of the hill.

This is the sort of occasion when a company commander requires a large supply of faith. The path-finder had now gone forward to "make certain of his bearings"; in plain words, I thought to myself, realise completely that he was lost. But his job was not easy, and so far, we had got on reasonably well. I decided to trust to him as long as I possibly could, told the men to lie down, and waited events. On Jackson and the mules, I dared not meditate, but reflected that at the present moment the last one could barely have passed the olive-tree.

After a few minutes the guide came back and said that it was "all right," he had found a way. He did not say he knew where we were, so I concluded that he was smelling out a new path as he went along. For the next hundred yards all went well; the slow, snake-like body of men behind me hoisted and wriggled itself painfully onward: it was taking time, but we were making headway. Every twenty yards we stopped, a safeguard against losing touch. If Job, who, I suppose, knew Judaea pretty well, had been one of the men of the leading platoon, he might have spoilt his reputation. But we had all graduated in Macedonia, and no one even swore. At the end of that break, we found we had got ourselves into a stone pound.

I grew rather cross. "Why," I asked, "did you take us this infernal way?"

The guide explained that the path was a long way round.

"What," I said, "do you mean to say that we could have been walking up a path? I don't care how long it was. It would have been far better than these beastly terraces. Look at us. What do you suggest now?"

He said that it had looked all right in the afternoon. We must have gone wrong further down.

I left the conversation suspended—hanging him, as it were, in the noose of it, and turned to the leading men.

"Take your packs off. Pull down that wall, and make a road through it. Is there an N.C.O. here? Oh! is that you, Bilkins? Good. You can take charge. Pass the word down. *To* Mr. Jackson *from* O.C. company: We're pulling a wall down."

I heard my message transmitted by four or five men with fair correctness. Then it came to a garrulous person who was half asleep. He took it to be an item of news passed to himself for comment.

"Here, wake up; the captain says he's pulling it all down."

"All right. When are we going to get to that blarsted hill?"

'Pass it on, it's a message."

"What's a message?"

"Job the captain's got on. Looks as if we've got into a hole."

I was about to stop this idiotic dialogue, when I heard a live message coming up the column. It was short and simple:

"Mule down. Halt in front."

A corporal refused to accept it. "Who's it from?" he demanded.

A pause. Then backward to the corporal came the flung reply. Again, voices were heard along the jumbled terraces: "Mr. Jackson—Mr. Jackson—Mr. Jackson."

"Poor old Jocky!" I thought, "he's having the devil's own time with the animals. If the end of the column's still moving, we must have strung out a good deal. Give 'em a rest for five minutes, and then get on!"

The men were working at the wall with great vigour. They, always like pulling things down. Bilkins was doing a double share, tackling the biggest stones, making comic capital out of pretending to be a strong man. I joined in to stimulate the rest. In a few minutes we had become accursed. We had removed our neighbour's boundary.

The men were roused up. Several minutes went by while we waited for the end of the column to realise that the head was about to move. Then the funeral restarted.

By good luck the expert who was guiding us now found four stones he had piled up one above the other during the afternoon. "We're all right now," he said. "I know those stones. They're mine. I put them there. We go up a bit to the right, and then a bit to the left. There's a wall there, but I made a hole in it. Then we go over a bit of flat rook—sort of pavement—strike a path—the old track you were talking of—and follow it into the next valley. Then . . ."

"All right," I said; "that's enough to go on with. I hope we shall get in by morning."

We gained the village, gingerly walked over the slippery face of solid rocky pavements that had known perhaps the feet—speculation fell as it fluttered backward to the past—and soon were treading a downward track. Lower and lower the path wound, rougher and stonier at every step. At length the descent was over, and we began to pick our way along the wide bottom of a valley.

We were now in a wilderness, the like of which I had not seen since the storming of the hills that cloaked Beersheba. Yet this was more rugged, more desolate. No vegetation that I can remember grew there except a few dark, scraggy trees at the further end, where the valley opened out a little, and joined the bed of another.

The track, such as it was, was littered with large pieces of rock, which lay about everywhere, as if the Titans had passed by in some dim period of the world's history and had had a pelting match. But the thoughts of some of us, as we stumbled on, stopped at the first years of the Christian era. If this was not in verity the "wilderness" of the New Testament, it was wild enough to form a background for events we had never been able to imagine against actual scenery.

I had always supposed wildernesses to be flat, empty spaces, confusing them, in my old down-at-heel way, with deserts. I had never pictured the scene in which I was walking: great hills with flinty bos-

THE WILDERNESS

oms throwing black sheets of shadow on each other, their inhospitable tops naked to the moon: hollows scattered with great stones, alleyways of darkness leading one knew not where, filled with immanent impersonality more personal than personality itself. This was "the wild," a place that only the devil could laugh in. We talked in whispers: became silent. My being was entirely centred in new contemplation of an old set of words:

Forty days and forty nights
Thou wast fasting in the wild;
Forty days and forty nights
Tempted, and yet undefiled.

I matched the whole conception against the life of a soldier. Practical details that would seem irreverent were they not so human forced themselves into my mind. Forty days must have seemed a very long time. Forty! my word!

Our new positions proved to be half-way up a hill that lay across the valley and at the further end of it. We had crossed the great ghost-like bottom, and were on a little path that wound upwards. This had been made by lifting the stones away and piling them up to a height of about two feet on either side. It was now time to branch off to the right, to reach that particular portion of the hill-side that had been selected for us. We dismantled a portion of our path's low wall, and in a few yards were climbing the hill's chaotic steeps.

After following for a little the violent bends and turns of a way that might once have been useful to goats, we came upon a flat ledge or terrace, with half a dozen low, roofless shelters of piled stone butted up against the back. Above this was another terrace, without shelters. Numbers of loose stones were lying about. Above, the hill rose steeply. About it, at various distances, shoulders of other summits lay in curved grandeur, black against the sky, or illuminated dimly by the moon. The place was empty of life: no stir of bird was there: the solitude was composed of the companionship of stone with stone. Our part of the hill lay in the moonlight. The men formed up as they arrived and then sank down. They were "done in" by the rough going. Warm for the moment, soon they would be bitterly cold.

The mules came up, the Lewis guns and all their complicated accessories were unloaded; in twos and threes and fours the men settled to rest. Going to bed was for them only too simple a matter. One after another the stone shacks were inhabited: bivouac sheets stretched in some instances over the roofless tops, in others kept for warmth, to cover more closely the bodies of their owners. I was doomed this night, it appeared, to share their chilliness, for the supercilious camel that had swung off with the officers' valises on its back had not turned up. Seeing the remoteness of our position, I should have been very much surprised if it had. The place was utterly unsuited for the entrance of such beasts. Their soft padded feet and easy, deliberate pace were alike unfitted for this hard, broken country. But their real troubles were not yet. And they were all we had.

It skills not, as old writers phrase it, to tell in detail my small personal tale of that night. By a kind of mysterious sense of direction with which neither Beattie nor his master was blessed, Jackson's servant, wandering in the hills, was led to discover both battalion headquarters (very snugly placed) and his master's baggage. Performing a prodigious feat of strength and devotion, he arrived, to fling it, like a good retriever, at two in the morning at his master's feet.

Aroused by his initiative, and following his vaguely pointing hand, Beattie and I set out at two-thirty (0230 hours, soldiers call it) on a similar quest. In twenty minutes, we found ourselves near some stone ruins, looking in the moonlight at a smashed machine gun, relic of some desperate encounter on the part of the Scots. At the same time, we became aware that a battery lay concealed in a compound on our right. A little further on the track branched off in three directions.

Both of us were tired beyond the spin of a coin: it was too late at these cross-roads to hazard another hour of wandering. We turned and plodded back to the position. Everyone had bedded down. The company fell easily into two portions, the housed and the houseless. The shacks were packed with men lying for warmth almost on the top of each other. Only the sergeant-major and the quartermaster-sergeant, twin pinnacles of that society, shared between them, a little distance away, one shack.

The remaining men of the company were lying about in the open. Their forms, wrapped up in sheets, looked horribly like the dead. Some lay on their backs, perfectly straight, as if they had been frozen there; others in constricted attitudes, as if they had been shot. I got over a low wall, and, swearing all the time at the adjutant, wrapped myself in my own sheets and coldly fell asleep.

Out of the confused memories of the three days—or was it two?—spent on these rocks, three matters of interest emerge: the shortage of matches, the arrival of a post-bag containing a newspaper whose bold headlines announced the collapse of the Italians, and our first sight of Jerusalem. Time has reversed the order of their importance, but if you then had asked any of the men, they would have ranked them thus—the dearth of matches, the "mess-up" in Italy, the sight of the city.

The contents of the post-bag interested the men deeply, for no one had realised up to now the gravity of the Italian defeat, and it was generally supposed that the true import of the matter had been kept from us. The sergeant-major held this view. He said he thought the newspaper had got into the bag by mistake.

This enormously increased its value as a piece of news, and it was passed eagerly from hand to hand and devoured by half the men of the company. Everyone was deeply impressed, and it was discussed seriously for several hours. But the present was so vivid and real to us, our interests so centred in our own campaign, that no news from Europe could permanently affect our minds.

It seemed like the report of a dream, something that was happening in another world. Let it all go smash over there, Palestine suns, handing over to Palestine moons their keepsakes of rocks and mountains, would still behold us stewing our handfuls of raisins over little fires at the close of day, mustering in our twos and threes for duty at lonely posts, marching, fighting, dying, obstinately determined to rid these hillsides of the tenacious Turk.

The clash of empires—"Armageddon" as some hundred newspapers have called it, carelessly firing away their one big shell at the very outset of the combat—cannot profitably long hold the minds of a community which has no matches with which to light its pipes. This reads suspiciously like the preamble to an advertisement, but is nothing but a simple statement of cold fact.

The smokers, that is to say, most of us, had scratched and puffed in thoughtless improvidence until disaster stared them in the face. It is ever thus with your Londoner, nicely obedient to the misinterpreted text *"Take no thought for the morrow."* Turn him loose in the desert, and he will first eat all his food, strike all his matches, smoke all his tobacco, and then bitterly complain of being left pipeless, fireless and unfed.

During the training period in England nothing could check his wasteful habits, and the remains of every meal he took, indoors or by the roadside, would have filled more than the Biblical twelve baskets. Experiences of a certain bitterness, elsewhere than in France, had checked a little the sublime carelessness of these city-dwellers, but even now they lived, in happy abandon, on the very edge of improvidence. Formed in another mould, with my spending propensities curbed in boyhood by the text "*What is not needful is dear at a penny*," accustomed to see about me thriftiness rather than waste, I came into the army with a more canny and possibly a less attractive character.

It is hateful to be without things, and to have to beg off one's neighbours. It was this provident strain that made me, in Macedonia, insist that my mess president should take up the line flour, suet, and treacle, rather than quantities of tinned pineapple, vermouth, and chocolate wafers. How well I remember purchasing the last sack of American flour in Salonica! Turned into suet puddings during a period of blizzard and semi-famine, it proved the most popular purchase the mess had ever made.

The match scarcity which has led me into these reminiscences took me by surprise. Moderately careful with my own—I had about a dozen left—it never crossed my mind that we were on the brink of an economic crisis. A non-smoker, previous match-shortages had never worried me; I had lived through them absolutely unaffected, and had even been able to relieve distress at the door—of my bivouac. My position—secretly discussed no doubt by the subalterns, who smoked like small chimneys—had always been considered impregnable. Surely suspicion should have crossed my mind when men of the company began to appear, asking Beattie if I would object if they took a light from my fire.

Next day these perpetual requests became a nuisance. The same night Jackson, a great borrower (he is still wearing a pair of my stockings and shaving himself with my razor), came up and asked casually if I could spare him half a dozen matches. I dipped into my box and pulled out about that number, remarking that I hadn't many left. Before we moved (there are several moves ahead of us), I went up to my old friend the sergeant-major, who was never "out" of anything, and said:

"By the way, you might let me have a box of matches: I'm short!"

He looked at me for a moment without speaking. Then, holding out his hand, he said: "Well, sir, if you care to take these . . . it's the last box in the company!"

Of course, I refused; then, conscious of a new dread, I looked for my own, and counted them. There remained *five*.

Such are the intricacies of narrative and the difficulties of marshalling and commanding masses of rebellious material that I shall probably never be able to allude again to this domestic trouble. Touched on cheerfully here (our rocky perch was not a bad place when the sun shone on it), it became during the next few days an ever-present worry. The crisis reached its height when the sacred flame of a single candle was all that was left to us. Had we at that time been cut off we should undoubtedly have settled finally into dark and fireless despondency. We might have been discovered by some runner, praying between chattering teeth for the arrival of a second Prometheus. But at this juncture, making my way one morning to battalion headquarters, I met a brother company commander.

"This match scarcity," I said, "is a very serious matter. There isn't one in the company." And I poured out my woes.

"Are you really hard up?" he queried, looking at me very suspiciously.

I almost choked with protestations.

Then suddenly (Poy was always the fellow for effect) he did the grand thing.

"Here's a box," he whispered. "Don't let anybody see it." Then, with a lofty air: "Have it, if you like. I don't want it." Finally, with immense satisfaction: "Got a private store, hidden in my valise."

This was the end of the great match question. Shortly afterwards markets became easier. Individual cases of distress were relieved in various ways. One runner in particular, waylaid by my scoundrels, was found to be a Lucifer. The crisis passed into the world of forgotten miseries.

I was discussing with the quartermaster-sergeant the mysterious disappearance of a load off the back of one of the ration camels—an accident, if accident it was, that meant the total and irrecoverable loss of all our jam and dates, when Jackson came and said:

"Coming up to have a look at Jerusalem!"

"Rot," I answered rudely. "Some old stone village, I suppose. Do you remember, miles away at Latrun, panting up that mountain on the off-chance, when a good look at the map would have told us it was absolutely hopeless? Glamour and excitement. Jerusalem's six miles away and comparatively down in a hole. Lots of higher hills in between."

"All right, if you *won't* look. The men want to go up. Do you think it'd matter if we let them, two or three at a time? I don't think we can be *seen*, though I'm hanged if I know where the line is."

I assented, and began to give in. A slight feeling of excitement came over me, though I held it resolutely down.

"Is it really there?" I asked—"Jerusalem?"

"Come up and see. You'll be awfully disappointed."

Together we scrambled upward: over little rocks and round big ones, trampling underfoot patches of low-growing, thorny furze. The summit I thought was a summit showed, as summits will, another summit, but at last I stood confronted with an expanse of country.

"There!" he said.

Far away, with one tall shaft standing by itself to the left, spread over a distant portion of the hills, lay a mass of buildings. It was evidently a town of some size, considerably scattered, seemingly built on no plan. A town, and an amorphous one, lying split among the hills, not pinnacled on high rocks, not, to appearance, walled, not, no, finally and irrevocably, not the city of my dreams.

I had supposed it small and compact, built like a castle, girdled by a great wall, a fortress city, with towers and bastions and turrets. And now . . .

"Thanks," I said. "It's a bit of a jumble, isn't it! I must come up with field-glasses and look at it again later."

Thus, passed the last of my childish dreams.

3: THE MOVE CONTINUES

This sub-chapter deserves several titles, for more than one subject comes within its narrow compass. I have been driven at last to put up with something noncommittal, have left it, in fact, a problem tackled but unsolved.

With slower pen men used to write
In Anna's and in George's days,

. . . . laments pathetically the lonely muse of Austin Dobson. Young men today cannot follow the precepts of Boileau, even if they would. The lives of many of them have been too full of incident: so much in strange fields has been attempted, so much laid aside, so many new things clamour for attention, that writing itself has to get on with the business and let French-polishing alone.

There are tales to be told, ready for the hands of cunning writers, but not to be cooed over, titivated, or played with. There are tales in the making, full of amazing problems, unfolding daily before our eyes. The future offers such tempting speculations, the present is eaten into so rapidly and affords to the art of writing such masses of appealing material, that it is an effort to turn away from it and gather and stack into books the late rich harvest of an immediate past.

Let me therefore not linger, but set the troops in movement. The troops! What pictures, glorious now and made immortal, float before my eyes! Motley crowds in England, stamping and shivering on "rouse parades." Battalions on English roads, marching in the spring-time, "fed up" with home-service and longing to be in France. The straight road to Arras and the same battalions, "fed up" with France and longing to be in England, but pulling themselves wonderfully together when they think they are going to the Somme and to destruction.

Again, under acres of canvas at the back of Salonica, men strung out like ants upon the mountains: and now again refitting at pleasant Ismailia; *anon* in columns of fours silently and stealthily in the moonlight going to surprise Beersheba. Troops!—ordered concourses of men, compacted for a great purpose.

★★★★★★★★★★

Our reserve position behind the hill did not long hold us in idleness. Indeed, it is probable that we owed the few days spent there, not to any desire on the part of the demigods to give us an easy time, but because the complicated series of reliefs then in progress required us for a few days to step out of the picture. A sudden notice to quit roused, though it did not surprise us. That sight of Jerusalem had brought back vividly into our minds the enterprise that had brought the division all the long way from Sheria. This constant changing from position to position meant that units were being rearranged for a purpose. In the transport, where all the low gossip of an army circulates, a whisper was born that we were moving south and would attack somewhere on the right.

This forecast, subject of many bets, was discredited when we learnt we were to relieve a company which for some days past had been leading an uncomfortable life on a back portion of the stony ridge which culminated in Nebi Samvil. When we had first relieved the Scots, Nebi Samvil lay to our right. For the last few days, we had it to our left fronts and were able to see, across a stony valley, one or two buildings of the village of Beit-Iksa, which lay between us and our first position. Between this village and Nebi Samvil was a hog's-back of broken boulders, high up, destitute of cover. This was the next position we were to take over.

Since battalion headquarters was some distance away, and the battalion itself split into widely separated units (I never learnt where two of the remaining three companies were stationed), we were given on this occasion a free hand to conduct the move when and how we liked. It was, in truth, a fairly simple matter, for there was a path as far as the village and the distance was not great. All depended on getting the other company commander to hand over his posts not a minute later than dusk, and so, in the afternoon, I went over with several guides to discuss this and other details.

Past the village the going was extremely difficult and we ran at an angle against several plots of enclosed ground and bits of the terraces that had proved such an obstacle on our last journey. A path that wound about proved no help at all, for so many big boulders had dropped on to it from the walls it followed, that it was practically impassable. An amusing place to scramble over in the sunshine, it would be horribly difficult by night, and particularly trying to the camels, who this time were to accompany us.

The guides, picked for the job, were careful to take in all these details, and were very busy piling up heaps of stones as landmarks, and partially clearing some of the more difficult passages. Every ten yards of this part of the road was discussed. The route was chosen, marked, and learnt. None of us, after the experiences of our last trek, wanted to waste time getting to the new position.

I found the company commander in a most miserable shack, surrounded by his adherents. He was very wretched, and poured forth immediately we were alone a bitter complaint on the ingratitude of princes. He said that the position was an awful one, not a vestige of cover, a battery behind us, enemy trying to hit it and constantly hitting his people by mistake.

"They're firing short," he said; "I wish someone would correct the range for them. Unless," he added, as a little shell arrived and burst in the rocks above us, "they've spotted us. Tell your men to lie close. You won't be able to put up any bivouacs. Can't take you round the line, it's too dangerous. There are half a dozen little posts. A machine gun comes up at night and sits down somewhere. It's a funny business. We're not exactly under anyone. Our orders are to guard the valley (where Johnny's got a listening post) and hold ourselves in readiness to retake Nebi Samvil if anything goes wrong. It might be well for you to walk over in the night and see them."

"Whom?" I asked skittishly; "the Turks?"

"The Nebi Samvil people. I can't ask you to eat anything," he continued; "sorry, we're short."

I would have given anything for a biscuit, but said that I was not hungry.

"No?" he went on; "lucky chap . . . I always am. But don't you think it's rotten of the brigade, after all I've done for them? On the Vardar, you know. All their bottle-washing. And they promised to make me a staff-captain. I *ran them*. And now look at me. Sitting in this beastly hole. Years afterwards. Still dragging these wretched fellows about—a *company commander!*"

"You'd like to get the relief over as early as possible tonight, wouldn't you?" I asked, trying to draw him off the topic.

I gained my point easily. The present had no interest for him. He was still bitterly conscious of his wrongs. "They sucked my brain," he reiterated, as I went away. "Goodbye; see you tonight. After all I did for them."

I quite agreed with my friend that night as to his estimate of the position. The relief was over. I had struggled round the posts at dusk with his company-sergeant-major. They consisted of a series of rifle-posts or stone sangars partly dug out of the ground, partly built up with large pieces of stone. They seemed to have been placed promiscuously, facing in various directions at different levels, and were a long way apart from each other. On a steep hill on the other side of the valley it was possible to make out in the dusk an irregular dark line—the Turkish trenches.

I did not like the idea of sharing this huge, many-terraced slope with the Turk, particularly if it turned out to be a dark night. The departed company had left behind it three graves, some old pieces of clothing, a sackful of damaged Lewis-gun magazines and a broken rifle, but I do not know if they were responsible for these relics.

That night was one of the loneliest and creepiest I have ever spent. Half an hour after the company we had relieved had disappeared a Scotch mist, wet, icy cold, and absolutely impenetrable, closed in on us. I had determined to go round the line early in the night, and started out, leaving Jackson at the lonely cairn that went by the name of headquarters. In a hole hard by, under a low, cock-eyed sheet pinned into position by four enormous boulders, my signallers had inserted themselves, like creatures that live under stones.

I found the first post, was directed to the second, and then spent two hours wandering on the hillside. At last, I came upon a piece of old trench that I remembered, and managed to get back to headquarters. Jackson was lying swathed in a blanket, his feet sticking out into the mist, for the cairn was so small that it did not cover us entirely.

"Well," I asked, "has anything happened?"

"The brigade-major has rung up three times. He wants to speak to you."

"Good Heavens," I thought, "I wonder if we have gone to the wrong place."

Crawling very flatly on my hands and knees, I managed to get into the "signal office." After many calls and much shaking of the instrument, it was at last pronounced "all right." The brigade-major was "on."

"About those hares," said a thin voice.

"Those *what?*" said I, absolutely amazed. "I'm afraid I don't understand, sir. There's a beastly mist up here," I added inconsequently.

"Do you think you could let me know how many you've got?" continued the voice politely.

"How many hares?"

"No, not hares," said the brigade major, "*flares*—red flares. We gave you a lot at Beersheba. Do you think you could scrape up fifty?"

Now flares, as my men soon found out, are, when properly dissected, good substitutes for fire-lighters. Beersheba belonged to the distant past. Even Sheria was becoming a dim memory. One or two of the men might have, as curiosities . , .

"Three," I said, clearly and decisively. "Only three. We counted them yesterday. You know what the men are . . . ."

"You'll have to find more than three," said the brigade major. "We've got to get them from somewhere. Ring me up tomorrow. Goodbye."

Morning was fine, with a chilly wind: it was followed by a night of intense cold. We had lain close, and with the exception of a fair number of shells, nothing had troubled us. The usual narrow escapes added a certain piquancy to life and conversation. The Turks were certainly somewhere about on the lower portion of our hill, for one of our advanced posts could hear them talking. Their trenches looked business-like. We wondered what sort of a fight they were going to put up for Jerusalem.

Jackson and I were unpacking a wonderful box which had come all the way from Alexandria—rice, chutney, glass-cloths, and candles, the remnants of an odd order given before the campaign had started, when I received a long message to the effect that the company was to be relieved. We were to go through Beit-Iksa, strike the "Roman Road," and at the other end of it, where it joined the main Jerusalem road, were told that we would find guides. Advance officers of the relieving company would come over during the afternoon. This looked like business. The news quickly ran through the company. Everyone was glad and excited.

Night came down again, dark and comfortless. There is nothing pleasant about moves at the best of times; this one would have to be conducted under the stars. The absence of the moon made me a little nervous about the negotiation of those difficult passages. Beyond the village unknown troubles waited for us. Various individuals in the company, turned on by sergeants to revisualise the way we had come, could not throw much light on that Roman Road, its turns and bifurcations.

But memory was all we had to guide us, for there was no time for reconnaissance. Mac, the much-enduring adjutant, who had been with us for so long, had lured me—over the phone, I think—into saying that it could be managed somehow, for one does not like to admit possible failure. Several men had been sent forward to improve the road and add to the number of those heaps of stones stablished to direct us.

The camels had come up in the dusk, and one hoped they would be able to reverse the process and get down again. These prehistoric creatures, who move their legs like pendula and gurgle when they are angry like the noise of water running out of a big bath, are absolute mysteries to me; I would no more think of looking after one than keeping a dragon. They came, led as usual by natives clad in long blue cotton robes, fellows whose devotion to duty and endurance of cold in these high latitudes deserved and obtained the admiration of their white fellow-soldiers. Mules, camels, and my own horse, "Marie Lloyd," that long-suffering animal, I handed over with a benediction to the stubborn Jackson.

"The tail of the column is yours," I said; "be happy with it."

"Anything you like," he replied, "only for Heaven's sake, don't go too fast."

"The pace," I answered, "shall be that of a funeral."

So, all in good fellowship, we went to our respective stations. I uttered the magic phrase "Carry on." The move began. Even the comfortable limits of a volume do not suffice when a writer's memory has the trick of reviving on inconvenient occasions masses of inconsequent detail. I could detail here the very turns and twists of the track for the first four hundred yards of this journey, and note the positions of stones and the tilt of the ground below.

At the same time, greater matters have escaped me, or are recollected only by an effort. Man, lord of the animals, is at the mercy of that developed consciousness which raises him above them. We write and remember, not what we would but what we can. Only rejection and the exercise of a little craftsmanship is allowed to us who call ourselves the masters. In a court composed of specialists, with psychologists sitting on the bench, it would be difficult to decide who was the real author of this patchwork book.

Very, very slowly, halting from time to time for no reason apparent to the men in front, we picked our way along the back of Nebi Samvil and through the village. The night seemed to be getting darker, but I was glad to reflect that this first portion of the move had been safely negotiated. Not without friction, however.

On several occasions, in the middle of a halt, the difficulties experienced by Jackson's menagerie came floating up to me in a series of heart-breaking entreaties: "We can't keep up"; "Halt in front, we're losing touch"; "The camels won't come on"; "They are falling down"; "We've broken in half," to which I would reply in various odd ways, according to my temper: "You *must* keep up"; "I've been standing still now for ten minutes"; "Damn and blast the camels!"; "Kick them up again"; "I'm moving on"; "Catch us up beyond the village."

Had we passed by this way before, or were we already treading an unfamiliar track? For more than a mile past the village I had been pretty sore of myself, glad to recognise in particular a footway leading over rocks that lay a-tilt. Then we had had a valley on our right, but where was the old notice-board telling us to look out for shells? We pushed on. It was now very dark. I began to think of holes and precipices. Then, suddenly, we felt the beginning of rain—no, not rain, but the rains, definite, calculable known buckets, whose first emptyings were coming upon us now.

In a few minutes we were struggling in a tempest through a mixture of stones and mud. We hoped it would leave off; no one dared admit to himself what we all secretly felt—that this was the beginning of the season of rains, rains that were going to keep on and on until they were exhausted. Not without warrant came into the Old Testament those phrases about the windows of heaven being opened, and the noises of the waterspouts, to which might have been added the gurgle of young torrents rising into tumultuous life in the *wadis*. The mist of two nights ago had evidently been the warning; doubtless the inhabitants had been getting ready for it for days. With rain came a

126

bitter wind and the darkness of impenetrable night.

We tramped on, hardly knowing where we were going, the pace gradually becoming more slow. We were all still clad in clothing fit for an Egyptian summer: no one had supposed, when the campaign began, that by the first days of December we should be moving about on these heights. There is one advantage about khaki shorts—you do not have wet stuff clinging round your knees. They have no other advantage. Most of the men's boots were worn out: further supplies were not forthcoming: the problem had been agitated time and again, but there was no solution; we did not even carry materials for repairs.

It would not have been so bad if we had been certain of our direction, but though I believed we were on the right road, I was not sure. After a few minutes a light came into view somewhere on the right, and I realised that we had sheared away from the valley and were in an open space. Glad to have come to someone who might possibly direct us, I stopped the column and went in search of it. A gradual descent led me out of the mud on to some rocks, and there, lying on its side, was a wrecked ambulance wagon. Inside, some men, though I could not see them, were evidently squatting round a candle. Lucky fellows, I thought, living in such a splendid house, and shouted:

"Hullo, there! where does this road go to?"

"Don't know," came back the disinterested answer.

"Don't care either," I said under my breath, "selfish bounders!" Then, in a very polite tone: "Do you think you could tell me where the Roman Road is? I've got a company here, and I'm not quite certain of the way."

"Never heard tell of it, sir," answered the voice in the wagon. "Ever heard of Romans Road, matey? No, sir, none of us don't know. Couldn't say, sir."

Feeling very much inclined to ask them why they were living in the wagon, and very angry at their stupid negative answers, I roused up the company, and we all began plodding on again. Before long I came to a place where the road (to which apparently, we had kept) split into two. At the same moment, from another direction, where there was no road at all, I heard a body of men approaching. Halting my own column, I went to meet the other, and ran straight into Lawton, one of our company commanders.

"Good heavens." I said, "where have you come from? Isn't this absolutely the limit?"

"Come from?" he repeated. "Well, I've come from that position you left three days ago. How, I haven't the slightest notion. The point is where we are going to. I hope you know the way. This *is* a piece of luck."

I explained that the road was breaking into two. "I know where we ought to be making for," I said; "that place where the transport were, under the trees, near En Nab. The question is, does either of these roads go there, and if so, which?"

"There's nothing in it either way," said he. "My mind's an utter blank. Let's go to the left."

After some discussion, which, in the absence of knowledge, led to no conclusion, we decided to follow his original suggestion, the two columns were melted into one, and the dragging march restarted. The track led us down a gentle slope which neither of us remembered ever to have seen before. Now that I had his companionship, and knew that mine was not the only company wandering in the darkness that night, I did not feel worried, but rather excited at the adventure, though sorry at the condition of the men. For the rain was still coming down in torrents, and the weight of their packs and wet bivouac-sheets and their general sodden condition made it very difficult for them to keep moving over the steaming ground.

In the last event morning, clearer-up of all mysteries, would come to comfort us. Lawton and I together talked the matter over again, and we decided that I should get on in front and see if there was anything to be seen. There was nothing to be seen but more tracks, running amongst more rocks. A period followed of short moves and long halts. The men said nothing, for there was nothing to be said.

At last, after about an hour, our track ran into a road of some pretensions, and shadowy forms of trees appeared on our right. It seemed to be very much like the plantation we were looking for, and yet it was a portion of it we had never seen. The hopeless nature of the whole quest now dawned on us, for we had never met anyone or seen the slightest sign of a guide. We had just decided to send small scouting parties up all the three roads in front of us, when an electric torch shone out, and a cordial voice said:

"Thank Heaven, I've met you. I came here on the off-chance. Biggs, go and tell the guides to come here. Poy's in; you're the last. I've been waiting here for ages. Why did you choose this road?"

It was Elder, who, in the intervals of having his septic sores attended to by various hospitals at Alexandria and elsewhere, used to come up the line and do odd jobs at battalion headquarters. Previously he had been second-in-command to various companies. But his forte was the execution of gymnastic exercises. He looked benevolent. He could not fight properly when it rained, because of his spectacles.

"We chose this road," I said, "because we had no proper instructions. Whatever you people at battalion headquarters are thinking about I don't know. Look at the men. It's disgraceful! How on earth did you think we were going to find our way on a night like this down to this infernal place? Where does this road lead to? How much further have we to go, and where are we?"

"It's nothing to do with me," said Elder, as we all trudged on. "It's Mac. We're all angry with him. I could have put all this right quite easily. It was absolutely necessary to have at least four guides, and he would only give me two."

"Well, we're here now, anyhow, so let's be thankful. Where's the battalion? In those trees!"

"Good heavens, no! This is En Nab. The battalion's at Kustul. You've come by the nearer road. It's about two miles."

"What's the place like?" asked Lawton. "Is it a good spot?"

"Trees—more trees. A sort of park. Tomorrow the battalion is going to take up an outpost position."

"If this rain goes on there won't be anybody fit to take up to it. What do you say to a halt, Lawton, to collect the animals?"

The senior member of the trio agreed; the men were halted and told that two more miles on a decent road would see it through, and we walked down to the end of the column. A few mules were there, but Jackson was not, neither were any of the camels.

"Why on earth didn't he send a message up?" I sighed. "I suppose he lost touch and took the other road."

Five minutes passed, and then, out of the darkness, a camel. It passed oh, rhythmic, antediluvian, accompanied by a slim native driver, bare-footed, his cotton garment clinging to his pitiful girlish figure.

"Someone will have to wait and collect all those beasts," said I. "Elder, can you spare a guide? Jackson will be all right. He's used to this sort of thing. Put a man at the end of each road, and we shall be sure to catch him."

With the fragment of transport that remained to it, the column now began to crawl forward. The rain was as vigorous as if it had only just begun. The road seemed very long. At length we saw, on the right, a dismal, flat-roofed building made of stone, looking like a small deserted farm.

129

"Brigade headquarters," said Elder. "Fine place."

We tramped on. A track bore off to the left, among some trees. We passed it. Our road began to go downhill. A few hundred yards on, an awful suspicion crossed my mind. Elder, I noticed, had not said anything lately, and had been looking about him a good deal.

"Elder," I began mercilessly, "do you know where we are? Where's that road through the trees you talked about?"

"A little further on," he said indecisively.

"How about that track we passed? Could that be it?"

"I believe it is," he answered. "I'm afraid we've gone too far. Sorry."

This conversation was overheard by some of the men. I dare not print their remarks.

It was the last straw. And yet, so much can man and beast endure, it broke the back of neither camel nor human being. Ten minutes later we were passing bivouacs. Morning dawned as, wet through and half asleep, we wearily erected ours.

CHAPTER 5

Encompassing the City

1: KUSTUL

On the eve of great events, when masses of men backed by long lines of transport are marching inwards, following, as it were, the spokes of a wheel to attack and capture the navel; when all that host is almost in readiness, and the horsemen are prepared, and operations can truthfully be said to have begun; when the enemy has led his best troops into the trenches and is prepared at all points stubbornly to dispute the passage of that inflowing stream; when the mind, passing beyond its own immediate concerns, reflects upon the divers activities so complex a host contains, a modern army and its myriad facets: sixty-pounders with their private wireless installations and heavy tractors, long strings of camels with their tireless blue-gowned attendants, planes high overhead with no chance of a safe landing if anything cause them to crash upon these rocky heights, ambulances with their casualty clearing stations in churches and monasteries.

The long backward ruck of heavily working transport (a world of experience in itself, unimagined by the troops in front), and finally, remote but very real, Kantara, the huge canvas town on the canal, the great repository and workshop which feeds and replenishes the whole:—when, I say, indulging in the wider view, one visualises and reflects upon all this, it seems a paltry thing to continue to narrate the doings of a few individuals, whose work, perhaps, did not matter, and whose presence or absence might not have affected the result.

But if our view is extended yet wider and we include in it, not only an army, or nexus of operations, but the Great War itself, which scarcely can be seized as a whole with its many fronts and fields of activity and nice gradations of what is military and what civil, the gradually growing world-reflecting bubble will at last waver and collapse, leaving us face to face with ourselves, the individuals.

So, as I cannot handle those mighty conceptions except after years of study, revisitings of localities, long hours in dry, heated chambers amongst maps and plans, diaries and memoranda, I choose the footpath way and follow the fortunes of a few, even though they have the ill-luck to be out of the supposed centre of the picture. In truth, I am chary now of estimating where the centre of natural drama lies, and wonder if it can be said to have one when any of the scenes can be conceived as the focal point of interest. My irksome wait in reserve, described in the second part of this chapter, may have influenced the very heart of events, for aught I know.

Perhaps a few troops at the head of the division coming up the Hebron road may have had an unlooked-for effect upon the defenders. God may put us all in the wrong, and prefer to follow the fortunes of a few privates of either side who did things (unknown to anyone) which could only be described as quixotic. Everyone I have ever asked who was even remotely connected with the affair has said it was his men who took Jerusalem, or without whose assistance the city would probably never have been taken. Many of them were the first to enter. A mighty company of Bill Adamses is growing up. Those who were not there say that there was no fight at all—that the Turks never seriously defended it. Every deep breath I draw reminds me of the contrary. I put in a claim for the Londoners. Hence this book.

★★★★★★★★★★

As morning dawned—the morning of the 7th of December—we perceived that we were in the hollow of two hills, on the outskirts of a plantation. The bivouacs of my company were pitched on a slight slope of very broken ground, rocks on earth, with a few bushes. At the foot of this slight slope, the ground was almost flat and the boulders were fewer. Here I pitched my own bivouac, on the edge of a small road which left the plantation at this point and passed, through an opening in two low stone walls, down and along the valley. On the further side of the road was a plot of ground, enclosed by stone walls, and in front of it a squat building, which looked like a tower, but turned out, happily enough, to be an old well, with plenty of good water.

It was all on a very small scale, but farther on, beyond the stone wall, the valley opened out. You could follow the road, which was little more than a track, for about threequarters of a mile, when, our map told us it bore to the left and joined the main Jerusalem road. It bore off, in fact, to avoid a hill, on the top of which a few stone buildings, of some pretensions and solidity, joined together and looking like a castle, were supposed to be a village, and were called Kustul. Looking from the edge of our plantation, Kustul itself could not be seen, but the steep, rocky hill on which it stood was a great landmark. Jerusalem was now due east of us, about six miles distant as the crow flies, and nearly double if you went by Ain Karim.

The rain had ceased during the last hour of darkness, and morning was fine, though cold. As the day advanced, the last clouds of vapour, remains of the storm, blew away, and a yellow wintry sun streamed down, sufficient to warm and dry us. The company was very tired, ignorant of what was toward, desirous only of being let alone. Neither officers nor men knew anything about the plan of operations. We guessed, but were not certain, that this was last or last but one of a final series of moves; our generals were ready, and something would shortly happen.

Many of us hoped it would not happen too soon. The transport rumour about being on the right seemed to have come true, but we were so ignorant that we did not even know how far our flanks extended. Everyone knew that the Fifty-Third Division were pounding up the Hebron road as fast as they could and were not very far south of Bethlehem. On the rapidity of their movements much seemed to depend.

While we were cleaning up and trying to feel less weary than we were, Temple came back. It was as if a pedlar had suddenly come amongst us, for he brought with him, good lad, combs, hair-brushes, studs, bootlaces, soap, a looking-glass, a pair of scissors—all the things Jackson and I were pining after. O, he had had a good time, rather. Been lucky in transport on the way down. Had somehow "wangled" an extra day. And he was feeling better—distinctly better. We, for our part, told the awful story of the wet trek. It was a pity he had been away, we said; he had missed one of the most interesting experiences the company had had, something really choice.

"The utter edge, wasn't it. Jackson?"

"Ra-ther. If Temple had been here, he would have fallen out."

"We would have left him to the beasts of the desert."

"He would have been captured by the wild men of the hills."

"Whereas," said Temple, "I was fast asleep in a lorry, and you jolly well wish you could have changed places with me. I might have fallen out, but I wouldn't have lost the transport—like Jocky."

It was ending, as some of our jokes did, in a regular bicker, when

Mac came round.

"Hullo, squabbling as usual," he said; "you'd better get all those things done up. We're moving. Did you forget that stud, Temple?" And he proceeded to give me orders for the company.

We were to hold Kustul: relief to take place at dusk. An outpost position. At present it was in the hands of one of the other brigades of our division. That was all he knew. "Can't answer any questions. Colonel suggests you go up in advance yourself and take a look round."

There was no time to lose. Beattie and I regretfully packed up and got ready to vacate as pleasant a spot as we had struck since our halcyon interval at Latrun. The little fireplace of blackened stones built against the rock-ledge, the shelf, carefully cleared and tidied, the dear well across the way and small stream that trickled from it—how sad we were to leave these tiny pleasures! The actual move was nothing.

A tramp of twenty minutes, a stiff climb, up the reverse slope of Kustul's small mountain, helped by a path of red earth constructed by the men who were holding the position, and we were at company headquarters, a few bivouac-sheets extending the natural shelter of a rock, closed in at the sides by walls of rough stone. I was instantly made welcome, and plunged at once into discussion. Those officers knew a good deal, and I eagerly drank in their news. The attack was to begin at dawn on the eighth. That would be tomorrow. Our brigade was to hold Kustul and adjoining heights. The other two brigades were to pass through us at dawn and take the main Turkish trenches.

The advance would take the form of a curve. The division would sweep north-eastwards towards Jerusalem on a given frontage of about two miles, touch the fringes of its eastern outskirts, and, crossing the Lifta road, wheel gradually to the north astride the Nablus road. Then, with this road as its new centre, the line would push due north and entrench at a point about four and a half miles north of the city.

I learnt also that our attack was timed to coincide with the arrival of the Fifty-Third Division at Jerusalem's southern outskirts. They would not enter the city, but push up east of it, joining our right flank. All this, I understood, was to be the work of a day. Our role was not plain to me. I did not know if we were to be used to attack the second objective or would be held in reserve to wait on events.

I gobbled up all this information, and began to ask questions about the position that would be mine the coming night. It was, they said, a queer one, and almost impossible to explain. The company commander would take me over the crest to have a look at it; Turkish guns would not shell a party of two or three. In the meantime, a cup of tea, and he would draw my attention to a few domestic details. Movement must be avoided bivouacs carefully sited under the lee of rocks; smoke from cookhouses watched and regulated. It was not a bad place, he explained—though last night had almost washed them off the face of it—but all those buildings just over the top would be obliterated early tomorrow morning by Turkish guns. O, we should catch it properly! He wished us joy. Thus, the company commander.

A few minutes later my host, myself, and the sergeant-major, who had made one of the advance party, climbed the remaining portion of the hill and looked around. It was indeed a queer place. First, we came to a small *mosque*, a simple room with a dome on it and one side knocked out. Now we had topped the summit and, scrambling over a slippery rocky platform, gained the shelter of a substantial wall. This ran into another, and both of them, reared upon the hill's forward face, made a kind of battlement, complete with strong-points and places for observation, entrants and re-entrants, until the original one straightened out into a mere wall again, and ended in becoming a field boundary, low falling on to the hill's left shoulder.

At several levels, and in different stages of decay, other walls led back from this frontal one and joined up in any way haphazard builders chanced on to what appeared to be the central remnants of an old fortress, now partly in ruins but containing many chambers, most of them built of stone, but some of wattle and dung plaster, all wedged together with doorways everywhere and unexpected courts.

Some of the odd low-browed rooms had quarrelled with the parent building and had established themselves, five hundred years ago perhaps, across a courtyard, to block it, or had gone in pairs to the wall, to spoil the view. It was very old and very primitive, and in the intervals of fighting down the ages had been given over to agriculture and to a handful of peasants who, with rough picks and axes, had shaped it a little to their peaceful purposes and stocked it with musty grain.

This was Kustul, important now, as formerly, as a strategic point, for below and away to the left the Jerusalem road could be seen, with high ground rising from the left of it and a small white guard-house at the left-hand corner where it passed out of view. Dropping one's eyes to the ground immediately in front of us, we saw that our hill fell steeply for a little and then passed easily into a flattish table-land, which continued for about half a mile with almost no slope, when it apparently came to a sudden end, but how sudden or deep the drop

: SKETCH · PLAN · OF · JERUSALEM · AND · ENVIRONS :

was we could not see. Glancing from left to right, I saw that this table-land continued almost level until it passed into an open valley.

The hill on which we stood broke away likewise in easy slopes to the right of us, until, half a mile to our right and a little to our rear, the ground gathered up into another hill, with a separate set of features. The horizon was broken by a mass of hilly country, behind which lay Jerusalem. But what made the view lovely was a place that gleamed white in the distance, lying low down on the side of a green and pleasant valley. Though out of our picture, for it lay three-quarters to the right of where we stood and was nearly three miles away, we at first forgot military questions and remarked upon its beauty. The likings of fond imagination hoped it was Bethlehem, but that village, though it lay in the same direction, was double the distance. We were looking, in fact, at:

The plume-like trees and buildings white
Of rock-hung Ain Karim,

. . . .a Russian colony, the most beautifully situated place I had yet seen in Palestine. This, and much else, we took in in a series of swift glances; here it can only rudely be indicated by rough words. I cannot convey the interest with which we consumed it or the contributory features of light and shade, colour and form, by which it was set forth.

It was not long before the positions of the various groups of sentries posted by night had been pointed out, and we were returning together to complete the handing over. By day the place was held only by an observation post, which lurked, invisible even to ourselves, amongst some rocks on the far edge of the tableland. Observation of a different kind was the business of various artillery officers who had camped in and about the building that I have called a castle. The place was stiff with them. One had taken possession of the *mosque* and had actually put up a camp bed in it. Such luxury and softness we looked on with contempt and disgust and secret envy.

Slightly to the right of our hill, in a depression which yet was part of the general high-lying country, we noticed that engineers were at work, building a low, squat structure. Iron girders were being lugged up to it: the work was being hurried on and evidently was of importance. Later I made inquiries. It was an observation post for the general staff.

The remaining hours of the afternoon were occupied in settling down and getting ready for the night. At the approach of dusk, I put out my sentries. The front was impossibly wide; on the right it did not seem to have any known boundary. I was told, vaguely, that there was another brigade in that direction, and that their left group visited our right one. On the left my responsibility extended to the Jerusalem road. This vast frontage was guarded by four groups, one in the middle of the plateau on the extreme right at the junction of two stone walls, the boundaries of fields; the second further back, in front of the big observation post; the third behind a central part of the wall that guarded the castle; the fourth down on the plateau again, in a field about three hundred yards from the road. Three of the four groups had each a Lewis gun. There was also a small listening post, in front of the right-hand post, and to the right of it.

Darkness seemed to come on more quickly than usual; we had but scant time to get the groups in position. The night was fine, though cold. The whole of my company with the exception of the posts were behind the hill, three-quarters up it. A plan of defence had been arranged, and subalterns and sergeants knew exactly where to go if the unlikely happened and the enemy should attempt in this quarter to forestall us or gain information by a raid.

This was unlikely, but the anxiety remained. It would be easy for the Turks to get through between the two hills, if they knew the locality, but the castle was a veritable stronghold. We more than half expected that directly the light was strong enough in the morning those ancient walls would be smashed to bits by enemy artillery, who were certain to recognise it as an observation post. Artillery F.O.O.'s (Forward Observation Officers), had to take that risk; it was part of their business. To garrison it would be folly.

While I was posting my men I was thinking about the attack. The troops were to pass through us about midnight: they had a considerable distance to travel before they could reach the Turkish trenches. Where the Turk lay, we knew not, but the guard-house at the corner of the Jerusalem road was his, and so was Ain Karim. The ground had been reconnoitred on the previous day; it had proved to be country of the utmost difficulty. Progress would be by rocky paths, and the men would have to advance in single file. At present there were a few clouds, and the moon was shining, but fitfully.

This, then, was the great show—coming off at last—and we would be out of it. No doubt we should have our bellyful before it was over. I was nervous of its success. The part of the Turkish position that I had seen—those rock-hung trenches on the precipitous heights near

Nebi Samvil—looked absolutely unassailable. The taking of Jerusalem! What a romance it was! And here was I, once a dweller in London, planting little bodies of men armed with machine guns on rocky steeps in Palestine, so that my piece of Judaea should be kept safe that night. I thrilled with nervous pleasure and excitement.

The men were posted; all, so far, was well. We had discovered a kind of loophole in the frontal wall of the castle where it ran out a little way and back again, forming a rough bastion or coign of vantage, and had placed one of our small guns there, to command the approach. With a ground-sheet rigged up over them, stretched by strings over that contained space, the team looked like a band of desperate fellows, determined to kill anyone who ventured to approach their stronghold. My Lewis gunners were always workmanlike, and though we cursed the train of mules that carried their paraphernalia, their value to the company was immense, and the four guns inspired us with a confidence out of all proportion to their actual value.

These ingenious automatic weapons, which had to be kept scrupulously clean if they were to be relied on when the critical momenta came; which were cared for and cosseted by their keepers almost as if they were lapdogs or toy spaniels, and fed exclusively on polished cartridges of a carefully selected make or brand, were considered by us even according to the mandate of a certain leaflet, as the company's own special section of artillery, an arm indeed to cherish and regard with affection. There was a post below us, to the left. One of the other guns was far away to the right. Well pleased with the way events were developing—the fine and moderately calm night, the peaceful settlement of the company into its new position, I retired to my bivouac behind the hill, and gave my two subalterns a few minor instructions.

I had not rested long before a slow creeping anxiety came upon me regarding our right flank. There was, I had understood, a brigade on our right, and we were supposed to be in liaison with it. Were we in liaison? Perhaps it was pure restlessness that made me suggest to the sergeant-major that we should make our way to the right-hand post and find out if any reports had been received. I did not know if he too was glad of an opportunity to be up and moving again, but he roused his great frame willingly enough on my appearance, and we set forth together.

It was a broken and complicated journey, but we knew the tricks and turns of the terraces pretty well by now, and it was not long before we received a challenge. Your Londoner is quick to twig a situa-

60TH ARTILLERY DIVISION IN PALESTINE

tion, whether his post is a piece of humbug created to placate zealous but ignorant authority, or whether it is a real, live job of work, and no threats of punishment will make him continuously vigilant on the one, or fear of hardship and danger anything but vigilant on the other. My men were alert, confident, but full of healthy suspicions. A corporal detached himself from a wall like a moving shadow. Then conversation in laconic whispers.

"Everything all right, corporal?"

I spoke quietly, almost in an offhand manner, though my teeth were chattering with cold and I was shaking all over with excitement.

"Anything to report?"

"No, sir. Can't get any information from the right, sir."

"There's a bit of a path at the back. Have you sent anybody up it?"

"Sent Blackmore—he's a reliable man—with Jingle. They came back half an hour ago. Came across several paths with large arrows on them, marked out in stones. Couldn't hear anybody."

"Listening post all right?"

"I was just going along to them when you came along, sir."

"Tell them O.C. company will be out on the right, reconnoitring. See you again in an hour. Come along, sergeant-major; we'll have to explore that path. I don't think we'll take anybody with us."

Making our way along the back of the wall, we scrambled out of the field by the far corner, stumbled over a beach of scattered boulders, and gained a path that wandered across the low saddle-back that joined Kustul to another hill that lay in a retired position to the right of it. For some little while we followed this path, till it led us off the saddle-back, and dropped quietly into a broad hollow.

Here it broke into two, one fork going down the hollow to the left to enemy territory, the other winding to the right, between the hill which lay nearest to Kustul and yet another, which now appeared in bare outline in front of us, sombre and desolate, sloping gradually up from the hollow's further side.

In the middle of the hollow or rocky bottom and about half-way along it we could see, as we turned to the left, the remains of a stone watering-place or old building. At our feet, pointing towards it, was a large stone arrow, carefully laid out in small pieces of rock. What did it mean? How strange to find this purposeful thing lying at our feet in such a solitude! Who, needing direction, had passed, or was about to pass this way? Then I suddenly remembered. Of course, the attack! This must be one of the places where they are going through. Tonight, or early tomorrow morning, troops will be filing along this path. Why is it not guarded? Who holds the hill in front of us?

An answer to these questions could only be gained by reconnaissance—that grand word, which, after all, does not mean much more than going out to look. To venture much further in the direction towards which the arrow pointed seemed to be beyond our role; to turn to the right and search about behind the line seemed fruitless. There remained the hill on the further side of the hollow in which we were standing, and perhaps it would be wise to tackle it, though it was far beyond our legitimate area. It was very worrying to find no troops where I had expected at least a post, and to discover that, apparently, the right of my company was "in the air."

"Same old tale," I said to the sergeant-major; "no information, no one making the slightest effort to keep in touch with us. How about that dark hill? I should like to know whether it is occupied. What do you say to going to have a look at it?"

He agreed, and we set off together, feeling, as we advanced, more and more lonely, and rather like bathers who cannot swim getting into deepish water. Every while and again I stopped, and the sergeant-major stopped, and we both stood very still for about two minutes, listening for sounds. All but the best posts generally give themselves away at even shorter intervals by some slight movement, a cough, or conversation. Higher and higher we climbed, and still the silence was absolute.

"I don't believe there is anyone here either," I whispered.

It was true. The hill was absolutely unoccupied. My mind grew easier, the tension relaxed. The hollow we had just come out of did not seem so awesome as we looked down on it. The part of it where we had stood was not visible, but we could see plainly in the moonlight the old stone building, or well. A foolish desire for adventure seized me—as if these nocturnal wanderings were not enough! I was filled with curiosity concerning the place. I longed to search it—to creep into its dark entrance. Were we not kings of the mountain, lords of this part of Judaea? I grew very bold, and spoke my desire out loud. Then, together, we descended.

My heart was in my mouth as we approached, but boldness was rewarded: there was nobody there. It proved to be a large shallow well enclosed by a small compound—that is how I remember it. But the place is not very clear in memory, in spite of the curiosity it engendered in me on the hill, and I can see myself much more plainly getting back down into the field by the gap in the wall where I had scrambled out, and altering the disposition of the right-hand post. There was a Lewis-gun team with them, and I sent this gun to take up a position near the well, pointing down the hollow. It seemed ridiculous to guard so huge a place with so tiny a weapon, but something had to be done. Then we breathed more freely.

The night was now beginning to cloud over, and on our way back to the company I felt a few spots of rain. Our position was very exposed and there was practically no shelter for us; most of the men on duty had of course none whatever. So far, the night had merely been unusually cold, a fact both of us had remarked on, for we felt it keenly in spite of our rough scrambling. By the time we were "home" again it was raining fairly stiffly, and there were signs in the sky that this was only to be taken as a prelude to what was to come. The cramped company area, our few ledges on the hillside, was already full of groping figures, making sheets more secure on the roofs of their shacks, or looking for heavy stones to weight the corners down.

From one or two quarters, where a fortunate owner had camped on a ledge where there was sufficient soil, came the familiar sound of the knocking in of wooden pegs, always a concomitant of tempest. A little gust of icy wind blew up, and died away as suddenly as it came. It was as if a master hand had lightly swept the keys of an instrument preliminary to a great piece. A bank of mist came drifting on, passed through us, and sped Jerusalem-wards, over the valley. Clouds, quite near to us, went hurrying by at a tremendous rate: a few minutes ago, they had been over the Mediterranean. But the sky had done with the publishing of this mighty act—if these were her couriers—and now was covering her face with masses of impenetrable vapour. I looked up. There was no moon.

Suddenly the wind came, blowing more and more strongly in short, tearing gusts. The rain, following a separate role, had steadily increased meanwhile, and now was falling in heavy sheets. Blackness hemmed us in. We were all drenched in a moment. Mud was everywhere. The approaching operations, battle, murder and sudden death, were forgotten in an instant. We had broken through with a shout into a more primitive state and were fighting the elements for the scanty remnants of our small joys and comforts.

And now, when an ordinary servant would have buried himself in his own shelter, Beattie appeared. Beattie the self-sacrificing and devoted, and wanted to know if he could be of any assistance. I could not refuse his help, and together we messed about in the mud and the dark, trying to prevent the ground my bivouac was pitched on from becoming a pool of water. It looked as if the contrivance would stick up, and that was about all. The subalterns, on a higher ledge, were in a worse plight, for they had foolishly constructed a kind of lean-to shelter by stretching their united sheets from the edge of a great slab of rock which lay with a downward tilt.

The forward corners of the sheets were supported on low poles, and the sides and front closed in by other sheets, pinned to the earth by large boulders. The water was now flowing in under the back edge of the roof. The sheet that served as a doorway still remained shut. I wondered how they were getting on inside. Silly idiots I they ought to have known better by this time.

Gradually, as the violence of the rain increased, the best shelters became leaky, the worst uninhabitable, and the whole company more and more miserable. I had no matches, and could not get any, and my electric lamp was hovering on the edge of death in a dull red glow. I had a candle, and six times the sergeant-major, who had a lighted one, tried to carry the sacred flame across to me in a biscuit-tin. At length we both gave it up, and I sat, wet, cold, and in pitch darkness, on a corner of my damp valise, wondering what to do next and how long it was going to last. Trickles of water were starting all about me, a sudden lick of wind might blow the whole shelter away.

My weary intelligence meditated upon this, and slowly framed a contrasted picture of my own comparative comfort and the shelterless condition of the men on duty. A resolution sprang up suddenly, born of a conception. I could do nothing, but I would go and visit them. Dashed if I would stay mumping under a wet sheet. I found the little group by the wall shrouded in ground-sheets, the sentry gazing intently into the rain. On my way back I missed the castle by following a wrong wall, but finally found it and visited my group there. The post by the Jerusalem road I funked looking for. A sergeant on duty who was up at the castle said he had been down there and that it was "all right."

On my way back, suddenly I had an idea. What the morning would bring forth no one could tell, but work and responsibility were bound to come, and to start the next experience, whatever it might be, with a certain amount of driving power and energy was absolutely necessary. At this rate I should be fit for nothing. The anxieties of the last trek had taken it out of me: already I was almost numb with wretchedness and fatigue. But if I could get dry and get a little sleep, then whatever tomorrow brought forth could be squarely faced. Then there were the subalterns; their energies, too, would be required.

Why should we not leave this howling hillside and get into the castle? Tomorrow morning it was going to be smashed to pieces. But at dawn we could get out again. The signallers would have to come too. I could install them in a room next to mine. Then we could run the show properly, and be ready for anything.

I told the subalterns; I told the signallers. All, naturally enough, were eager to assist; moreover, the signallers had sufficient spare wire. Telling Beattie to take my bivouac to pieces and roll my valise up in a groundsheet, I climbed up over the hill and plunged into the castle. Even this simple act was not easily accomplished, for the dark night and wild weather made the finding of it a matter of infinite care and attention. But certain rocks served as guides, and once the *mosque* was hit upon, we could find our way to the ancient building. Half falling over great boulders that lay about in the courtyards, and stepping into pools of water where the pavement had given way, I discovered at last two chambers suited to my purpose.

They were slightly below the level of the yard onto which they gave, but stone sills to the doorways kept the water from entering. These entrances did not face the outpost line, but were at right angles to it, a great advantage, for I had conceived the idea of lighting a fire inside one of them, and was afraid that the glare might be seen. There were no doors, but a sheet could easily be rigged up as a screen. Here at last, for an hour or two, I could enjoy a little peace and privacy, reorganise my domestic affairs and rest my whirling brain. For none of these things were conceived in a spirit of tranquillity. A demon of excitement and anxiety had entered into me, and the vision of the attack was constantly before my eyes.

I knew that the division was committed to it, but could not conceive how it could possibly be carried out as long as this tempestuous storm raged. How could any troops find their way anywhere in such a night? They would be projected forth, I supposed, keep direction for a few hundred yards, and then fall into a ghastly confusion and perhaps fight each other. No, it would be cancelled. It would have to be postponed. It could not possibly take place. But what if we were deeply committed and could not draw back? Even now a division was struggling up the Hebron road to join hands with us.

What a night for them! I saw their transport floundering in the mud, axles breaking, teams of plunging horses disappearing suddenly with their following loads into some gulf that dropped sheer from a road that took a sudden bend. Then it was all blotted out and my own company took the stage. What if the night were dark? I could see, as by a series of quick lightning flashes, the mountain where I had stood in the early part of the night, my wretched sentries stationed on the plateau, and the plateau itself, wet and desolate. I clenched my teeth, and threw it all away, driving myself to attend to the immediate work that waited. Such small affairs—the sheltering of a miserable half-dozen—yet even this demanded planning and contriving and the strong hand of a ruler.

Before I left the castle and found my way back to the company my plans were laid. There was a third chamber, two more, in fact, on the other side of the small courtyard, and I had explored both of them. To reach one you had to go up a short ladder. It was a kind of barn. The other, a smaller one, was more accessible. I would offer these to the subalterns. It was unsocial of me, no doubt, even unkind perhaps, not to have them with me in my own chamber, but the polite and civilized part of me was worn out, and I could not stand them.

My servant—yes. The other officers—decidedly no. I knew what it would be, how it would all end if I let them in. Tired and wet and disagreeable, they would come fussing about and, as usual, quarrel with each other over some ridiculous trifle—the exact allocation, say, of the remains of a pot of jam. I could not and would not be a witness of that sort of thing on such an occasion. There was plenty of wood if they were enterprising enough to look for it. Let them light their own fire and bicker and scrap at a distance.

It took more than an hour to complete these simple arrangements, for darkness and storm added a thousandfold to our troubles. Runners sent up to the signallers, who themselves lost no time in getting off the hillside, disappeared completely and did not arrive at the other end until long after they were required. No one, setting out singly, seemed to be able to get to the castle at all. Some went to the *mosque* and stayed there. Some wandered out in front of the line. Everything any of us attempted during that awful night seemed to end in error and misconception. It was still blowing and raining when I led Temple and Jackson into the courtyard and said:

"There you are. You can doss down in either of those two rooms. This is the signal office. And I'm going in here."

"Can't we go in with you?" asked Temple dismally.

"No," I said, and I felt every inch the utter beast I was. "I'm dead tired, and I'm going to have this room to myself. Sorry. It's got to be.

They're good places," I ended up; "if I hadn't had the idea, you'd both have stayed on the hillside."

They pushed off, and I plunged with Beattie into my new apartment.

Revealed by the light of a candle lit by matches produced by the signallers, this room, with its shadowy walls and roof held up somewhere in the darkness, was heavy with personality and with the past. We might blunder into it, but we could not by the mere stamp of a modern field-boot exorcise the spirit or troop of spirits that dwelt in the place. There was something that made us feel venturesome as we went in. We felt that we were destroying old privacies at every step and laying ourselves open to punishment thereby.

There was grain in one corner of it, heaped at the end on a slightly raised portion of the boulder floor. An extraordinary upright affair made of wattle and daub was the only furniture; it had been used, perhaps, for the storage of meal. Those portions of the roof we could see were built of vaulted stone, but the middle part of it had evidently collapsed at some distant period, and now was supported by a large, shapeless pillar of stone, which stood in the centre. The roof was high, the architecture rough and uncouth. On most parts of the boulder floor chaff was lying.

It was not long before a wet ground-sheet was rigged up over the doorway and I had swept a large area of the floor clear of chaff and started a fire in a circle of protecting stones. There were some old pieces of wood in one of the dark corners. They were as dry as tinder and burnt splendidly. The flames leapt up and revealed the rest of the roof. It was flat, made of rough branches covered with a kind of furze or heather that served as thatch and was apparently weighted down on the outside by stones.

Indeed, at one corner they had proved too much for it, and the rough timbering had given way and remained hanging at a dangerous angle. Afraid of setting fire to it, I smothered the blaze a little, wondering how long the roof would hold. It must have been tremendously thick, for no water had come through. It had probably been hanging like that for ages, but tonight it must, I thought, be heavy with water, and I kept on glancing up at it, to see if any change had taken place.

My plans, which were entirely selfish, were to dry my clothes and my bivouac, which had been dragged up desperately by Beattie and dumped down on the floor, a large, unmanageable bundle of soaked stuffs, then have a good meal, and finally a wash and a shave. Headquarters were on the left of the road on the other side of the hill, doubtless fighting the hours of darkness in their own way, and miserable enough too; I would tackle events in mine, in that shadowy room. The first thing was to make some hot cocoa in Seattle's mess-tin, and some porridge in a flat, round cooking-pot, my most treasured possession.

Then the event of the night would take place, the frying of two rashers of bacon, one Beattie's and one mine, for he and I pooled rations and shared everything. This bacon Beattie and I had saved up for the last two days, waiting for a chance to cook it with due ceremony and eat it with enjoyment. The arrival of such an unexpected item in the day's food consignment had created a tremendous sensation, and the news had quickly spread throughout the whole battalion that bacon had "come up." We Londoners had soon got to know somehow that the Fifty-Third Division, which clung to the Hebron road, had been feeding almost continuously on this luxury. Such, at any rate, was the rumour. Many were the maledictions hurled at our own toiling supply column, and bitter the remarks passed about the softness of some fellows who didn't know how to live on "mobile rations."

I had determined to keep the fire going all night, and to do this a good supply of wood was necessary. That which we had found in the room was already nearly burnt up. Early in the afternoon, when I had been exploring the castle, I had found a chamber on the other side of it, with a low-browed door. To get to it you had to climb over a wall and jump into a courtyard which stood on a lower level than mine. Inside the chamber I had found a very large quantity of faggots; in fact, it was packed solid with them almost to the door. They had retained the heat in an extraordinary way, for the place struck hot though a cold wind was blowing outside.

I now set out to look for this room, but, do what I could, failed to find it. After climbing several walls, and once rolling off the top of one into some ruins, I lost my temper and swore I would take what I could find, wherever it was. In a little round house, I found a small heavy pick with a short stout handle. Banging around with this in my hand, I presently came upon an old wooden door. This I wrenched from its crazy hinges, and, still clinging to my pick, struggled back, lugging the door, somehow, with me. The fire was burning merrily, and I at once began smashing up my trophy. I was standing on it, slashing away at it with the old pick in all the gladness of demolition, when Jackson appeared.

"Well," I said, rather guiltily, "how are you getting on? Good bit of wood, this. Have you got a fire going!"

"No," he answered, "we haven't." Then, after a few moments spent in looking about the room: "Ours is a rotten place. Can you give us a piece of candle!"

Candles were very precious in those days. I took a reserve piece, measuring about four inches.

"If that is any good."

"Can you spare it?"

"No. Take it before I change my mind. Look here, I'm coming over with you."

We crossed the courtyard together, both stepping into the deep puddle of water just outside the door. As we did so, I decided what to do. We reached the other room. A guttering candle was there, running the last moments of its life to waste. Up against a wall sat Temple, his knees drawn up and his eyes closed. A valise lay on the dirty floor.

"Well," I remarked, "when are you coming?"

"Where, skipper?"

"Over to my room. I've got a ripping fire, and there's plenty of cocoa. Buck up."

"It's awfully good of you."

"Rot. I was a beast to tell you to come here, but I was so tired that I hardly knew what I was doing. Just for a moment, you know. Now I feel like a lion."

Three-quarters of an hour later I was again squatting quietly by the fire in the vaulted chamber. The meal was over; we had feasted together, gloriously. Beattie, as silent as a shadow, from time to time moved the sheets as they gradually steamed into dryness. Over in the raised part lay Jackson and Temple, fast asleep. Temple was lying on a soft bed of grain in an attitude of utter exhaustion. His face was turned towards the fire and I could note all the features, the proud nostril, the sensitive, petulant mouths He was white-skinned and as delicate as a girl. "He never ought to have been out here," I thought; "let him sleep now, he'll want all his strength tomorrow."

The night wore on. I listened to reports from runners, washed myself in water from a hollow in the rocks outside, shaved, and continued to tend the fire. Sometimes Beattie would look out and report upon the weather. The wind had died down, the rain had turned to a fine mist, everything was very still. Many runners had tasted many brews of cocoa, and the sergeant-major, who had been round the posts again, had dropped in and had had a meal. Now my famous fire had burnt to a great mass of red embers, and the walls had fallen back into gloom.

Thoughts chased through my brain, and in this quiet period of indeterminate night I visited many places, went home on leave, took the company again up to the line in Macedonia, went sick, and lay in hospital. Then the tumultuous present would break in, with all its problems. The attack. What was happening? Had it all been shut down? If it held good, surely that righthand post would have reported something. It was past midnight now. Dawn would be upon us before very long. And the castle scene would be ended. There was that bombardment. It would never do to fall asleep. We should have to get out of this.

A sergeant came in.

"Number one post report that the attack's begun, sir. Men have been passing through the line for half an hour."

"Quite sure that they are our men?"

"Quite sure, sir. They were making for that village on the right. Ain Karim, I think they call it."

He left me reflecting. Our job, which had been to cover this advance, was now practically over. It was about one o'clock in the morning. The sooner the men could be collected the better.

But the signal office were unable to put me on to the adjutant. The wire was broken. I pitched into them for not letting me know. How long had I been up here cut off from anyone? Half an hour! Three-quarters?" Why don't you report these things? Suppose anything had happened. We should have been dished—absolutely dished. Now when is it going to be put right?"

A tired and comfortless-looking operator, his head covered with what appeared to be the remains of a large woolly stocking, told a vivid tale. According to him, whole sections of our line to headquarters had been cut out and stolen by some neighbouring artillerymen who were hard up for wire.

"We have been out all night," he said, "trying to find the ends, and when we did mend it they took some more from another place. I can't understand it. We have never had such a job before. It must be the artillery. Two of our chaps are out on it now."

His candle threw a little light on the bodies of other signallers, lying in various attitudes hunched up on the floor, all with woolly stockings on their heads, all, apparently, worn out with trying to cope with the artillery.

"We shall have to clear out of this before dawn," I said. "How long do you think they'll be!"

He thought half an hour, and I mentally doubled his estimate, and left him. The mist was everywhere. I went up to the Lewis-gun post that kept the castle, and talked in low tones about the attack to the man on duty. Somehow the hour went by, I rang through. Permission to move the posts was not given.

"Nervous blighters," I said to myself; "I wonder if they realise what sort of a night the men have had, out on the plateau."

At the end of another hour, I decided to chance it and start preliminaries. The castle would serve as a rendezvous. I sent runners out to tell the posts to come in, and to do it quickly. Before long, it would be morning. Mists are deceptive and not to be relied upon for cover. Now was the time to make everyone brisk and decent. I roused the subalterns and told them to go to the company and get the men to pack up and be ready to move. It was a hard task. Tired out and wet through after the long hours of night, the men moved slowly and mechanically, scarcely seeming to know what they were doing. It was a dismal and depressing business, but the company had to be pulled together somehow.

Most of the men were collected in the castle, when a message came from headquarters that I was to close and move as soon as possible on to the road. This meant that the way down had to be reconnoitred, for we had come up from a slightly different direction. Those mules would have to be got hold of. The camels would reappear. Some of them, I had heard, had spread-eagled themselves during the night by slipping on the mud and were dead. There was any amount of work to be done. If only someone could make these fellows get a move on. The mist grew whiter and whiter. From far away came the sound of rifle fire.

My last party disappeared over the hill. An artillery observation officer had been worrying me for the last ten minutes to get them off. Slowly the mist rolled away until the tops of all the hills round were visible. The rest of the country was hidden, and remained hidden. There was a silence, strange and uncanny when the noise of many guns was expected. But few guns saluted the dawn that morning, and none in my section of Judaea. The bombardment of Kustul never took place, and the castle-village and its old vaulted chamber stand today.

2: A Position of Readiness

There is no time for prefatory remarks as the closing scenes of this narrative are ushered in. The long drama of our coming to the city of Jerusalem is almost at an end, the climax near at hand. From this time onward the tale will never stay for an instant, but with eyes that stare ahead sweep straight to its goal. If when print has done its cold business these symbols, read silently and thus bereft of the added appeal of voiced harmonies, contrive to quicken the imagination of one quiet auditor, they will not have been traced in vain. The choir of singing men and women, ancient and modern, young and old, performs for sympathy rather than self-satisfaction, and values appreciation better than golden coin.

If you can but march with us, if you are still by our side in these adventures—you had a right-Shakespearean invitation at the outset—we shall be contented though all the time you have been reading in borrowed pages. It is your imagination we want; the request is nearly as ancient as the hills of Judaea. English men and women are never slow to give it when the work is broad based, simple in execution, not peculiar, sectarian, or affected. A dealer in perishable ware may be humoured a little when he remarks upon the durability of the articles he offers for sale. But all this is so much whispering in the wings, and look, up goes our curtain.

★★★★★★★★★★

The company, wet and tired and draggle-tailed, were formed at last in a ragged column on the road to the left of Kustul. This represented a genuine achievement on the part of everyone in authority, for a little while ago it had seemed that we should never be able to get away from the place where we had spent so uncomfortable a night. The trouble had been equally shared by the men, the mules and the camels. The men were so sluggish that I thought we should never get them down the hill, the mules and camels found the ascent so slippery that we could not get them up. They waited for us in the road, and all the Lewis-gun limber had to be man-handled down to them. The beasts looked on, as miserable as the men. But night was over, and at last we had got away from that hill.

The battalion, a runner told me, had moved a few hundred yards up the road, not in the Jerusalem direction. So, we about turned, and setting our backs to the uncertain conflict now being waged beyond Kustul, pulled ourselves together and sloshed slowly on, looking for the other companies. After a few minutes the road forked. The left prong, a mere track, bent off in a southerly direction, the other, the main road, bent slightly to the right. The lie of the land through which this main branch now ran differed considerably one side from the other. To the left the country was open. First, if you quitted the road you would cross a large flat field covered with big boulders. This rose gradually to meet a series of enormous steps, each an acre or so in extent and about five feet above the one below.

To the right they ran up into a hill, to the left fined off to meet the track. But on the right of the road, and slightly below the level of it, a quaggy piece of waste land that had once been ploughed extended for several hundred yards, long and narrow, a mixture of weeds, grasses, and rocks, on a general background of red sticky clay. It was narrow, for further extension northwards was blocked by a confusion of rocks—a hill, in fact, adorned with the usual assortment of clefts and terraces, whimsical tipped fragments and areas of open face. In this field battalion headquarters and the other three companies had forgathered, and were now taking wet comfort.

The weather by this time had cleared. A wintry sun and a keen wind were working together to obliterate the effects of the previous night, but our sodden field was very much as the storm had left it. Everyone shivered and idled about, wondering what the next move would be. The men were told to hold themselves in readiness to fall in and be marched off at any moment.

For the first hour the prospect of movement and excitement kept us from boredom, but by the time it had lengthened into two, speculation as to the progress of the attack—our only topic of conversation—died for lack of nourishment, and we were left, cold, wet-footed, miserable and silent. Those also serve who only hang about, but it is a form of service not popular among men of action.

"If only something would happen," said Temple, who was always colder than the coldest, "I would welcome it; even a fight would be a change, and I hate fighting."

I proposed a walk along the edge of the road, to get warm. Then I noticed a ditch that ran half-way across the field, and we got into it, and squatted on our hunkers, to get out of the wind, which cut like a knife. But the ditch was wet, and discomfort drove us out. We parted then, and I made my way to the hill and started climbing it, examining all the rocks. Finding this kept me warm, I continued to ramble about it for a long time, keeping the battalion in sight below. By this time the road was silting up with transport proceeding in the direction of Jerusalem. I felt horribly out of it and cursed the ill luck that had doomed us to be stuck here while the city was in the act of being taken.

Movement began to take place among the men on the field. Certain that we were off at last. I rushed down, to find that they had all been victims of one of the many false alarms that keep the nerves of

reserve troops always on the stretch. Then we fed. It was the scratchi-
est of scratch meals, for no one dared start cooking anything when
any five minutes might give us our marching orders. Early in the
afternoon various odd men coming down the road began to bring us
rumours, all different, about the attack. Some said we were held up.
"You'll be for it soon," said another. A third said that all the Turkish
trenches had been taken, but that the London Irish had lost heavily.

More than this no one could tell us, but one thing seemed certain,
that though the main western defences had fallen in the early hours of
the morning, the Turks had not yet been squeezed out of the city. No
one could give any news of the bacon-eaters, the lords of the Hebron
road. A passing officer said he had heard that they were "hung up" at
Bethlehem.

Our attention was diverted from these matters and from ourselves
by a battery of sixty-pounders, which now took down the shutters
and opened shop in fine style on the lowest but one of the terraces
on the other side of the road. It was exhilarating to see them shooting,
and everyone began to take a kind of second-hand credit for it. Deaf-
ened, we became more cheerful. Our part of the world, at last, was beginning to influence events. Where there is a battery there is firewood.

Handing over the company to the joint care of Temple and Jackson, I strolled off, with the double object of having a closer look at
the guns and getting fuel. I found them ranged along the terrace,
great mustard-coloured fellows, shrouded in nets and bedded down
on sand-bags. The officer who was controlling the battery was sitting
in the centre, about fifteen yards in rear, getting orders over a phone
and singing them out through a megaphone to the gunners.

The guns had a tremendous recoil, and jumped considerably in the
act of speaking. The whole affair was splendidly managed, going on
calmly and quietly, though the guns were working at high pressure.
I felt part of a very inferior show as I watched this row of splendid
machines in action. It was like a ship commanded from a quarterdeck.
No trouble about communication here. How different the problems
that beset a company!

I voiced my timid request and was directed to several caterpillars,
the horses of these guns, which had come to rest on the other side of
the track. I have often wondered what the natives of Syria thought
when they first saw these queer contrivances crossing the desert towards Gaza, with their large supply tanks and top display of moving
wheels and parts, all rattling and whirring together, while the machine

itself crawled forward at a snail's pace. But however humorous or terrifying their aspect to civilized or uncivilized man, it was in no small measure due to them that we were in this part of Palestine, and not entrenched for the winter on the line of the Wadi Hesi.

On my return I learnt that, as no further orders had been received, we were to bivouac for the night where we were. The men fell in and the companies moved to various positions remote from the road on the lower slopes of the hill. I had just chosen mine, which was quite a little distance up it, when I suddenly saw our field ambulance making, apparently, for the same spot.

"Excuse me, this is my ledge," I said, as they came up, "but I dare say there is plenty of room for both of us."

It was easy to come to an arrangement with these good-tempered officers, who were equally popular with every battalion in the brigade, and in a few minutes, we had settled down side by side. I had not seen them since the day we came to Latrun. I little thought how deeply I should be indebted to them within twenty-four hours.

We had scarcely got our bivouacs up before the rain recommenced. Not in floods, as on the previous night, but first a cold drizzle and then a steady downpour. It was intensely cold—colder than I had ever experienced it in Palestine. The talk of the camp and all the business of it centred on rations. These had failed to come up, but until they had been distributed no one could get any rest.

There was a strong rumour of an early rouse up in the morning, and rations had to be issued before we started. We did not wish to repeat our experience at Sheria, where we had to leave part of them behind for lack of time to complete the issue. I well remember looking regretfully on that occasion at half a sack of sugar and an unopened case of bully-beef. But there had been no time to distribute it and no one to carry it, and we had had to hurry away.

It was sickening to think that after spending a whole day in doing nothing we should have to sit up half the night. From time to time I made inquiries. The answer was always the same. At length, about midnight, a portion of them arrived. Then there was another wait. The night was pitch dark, and the issuing was a matter of extreme difficulty. Fragments of conversation kept coming to me and mingling with my dreams as I lay screwed up, covered with everything I had, and yet icy cold. A corporal seemed to be having a lot of trouble with one of my four Joneses.

"Jones B. T." (bang at the tent). "Have you got your biscuits?"

"This isn't Jones, corporal. He's further on. Mind the string."

"Has everyone got his biscuits except Jones B.T.?"

"Here you are, corporal. I'll have some."

"You shut your head, sonny, or you'll find yourself loading the camels tomorrow morning."

"All right, corporal, I'm coming." (*Crash.*)

"Look what you've done, you bloody fool! Gone and bust our bivvy."

"Is that Jones B.T.?"

"No. I'm Jones F. Jones B.T. went to hospital this morning."

"All right. I don't want you. Is there anybody in number eleven platoon who hasn't had his issue of biscuits!"

As the discussion showed every sign of reviving and I wanted to get some sleep, I now broke into it in a loud voice:

"Look here. Corporal Huggins, I don't want to hear any more to-night about number eleven platoon or the Joneses or their biscuits. Have practically all the men got most of the rations that have come up?"

"Yes, sir."

General titter from the neighbouring bivouacs.

"Then go and get some rest yourself. Goodnight."

"Goodnight, sir."

But it was no use trying by the utterance of that soothing word to still the camp's unrest. Now dates held the supremacy. Now the quartermaster-sergeant had mislaid a box of bully-beef.

"I know it came up," I heard him say. "I counted them."

Then the voice of the sergeant-major:

"I expect you've issued it, Jack, and forgotten about it."

At about three o'clock in the morning our attempt to get a night's rest was finally dispelled. The order went forth that we were to move; we were wanted, and wanted quickly. Half-past three was the time fixed for our departure, but preparations dragged on and on. It seemed impossible to get the men formed up. A tempestuous and windy dawn was slowly glimmering into day, and yet the battalion was not ready.

Two out of the four companies had been got together, and were waiting, just visible, a little way off the road. My bivouac had been packed for a long time, but there was no sign of either the mules or the camels. Jackson and Temple themselves had been very slow, but now we three officers were engaged in the pleasant task of slave-driving.

"Come along, Aylott; get that bivouac down."

"Stop messing about with those tins, you, there, and put on your equipment."

"Jingle, are you ready to fall in? You are? Then help those fellows over there with the Lewis-gun stuff. Quick, get a move on!"

"Whose bivouac is this, still up? Thunder and Egan, I suppose, the old firm. Peters, who are you grinning at! Kick those pegs out, all three of you. Give you four minutes."

Bit by bit, four small parties of men, all that sickness and Sheria had left of four platoons, came together and were welded into one. Here were the mules, coming at last. Poor blighters, what a sight they looked! And here, too, was the colonel, riding about like a two-year old, smacking his legs impatiently with a riding-crop.

"Your company is bloody late. You're keeping the battalion waiting."

"I'm very sorry, sir."

"Order of companies. A, B, D, C. Rear parties will be left to load the camels. Lead on."

Slowly the four columns disengaged themselves from the slough in which they were standing, and wound in turn on to the Jerusalem road. It was good to be in movement, to feel something comparatively hard under one's feet again. The rain had ceased, and though full morning had not arrived, the day promised to be fine. We headed towards Kustul, left that memorable position on the right of us, and took a downward road. We were wanted at last, we were going up, perhaps we should enter Jerusalem.

Those who were out of step got right with the others, and something of the jaunty swing of long ago came back into the march. We were on the way now, going towards that white guard-house I had seen from the hill of Kustul. The road took a bend at that place and disappeared from view. I had longed then to be able to explore it and see what it was like round the corner. Before long, my curiosity would be satisfied.

SURRENDER OF JERUSALEM

CHAPTER 6

The Great Day

1: HOW WE CAME TO JERUSALEM

If this last chapter fail to bring again into reality the scenes it dwells upon, the experiences from which it is drawn are not at fault, but the commander of the company whose adventures are here narrated. The book, indeed, would not be ending now, were it not for a certain unlucky card dealt by fate to the author, of which something *anon*. This series of marches and dry and wet experiences would have formed, had the fates been kinder, the third of a set of four volumes.

The first would have described the raising of our unit, its long sojourn in England and France and our adventures there. The second I would have devoted entirely to Macedonia, a country that well deserves a book. The third is almost accomplished—it is unfolding before your eyes. But the fourth, the sad and disastrous fourth, where our little epic found its climax, alas! the greater portion of it would have to be completed at second-hand.

Thank God I am alive to tell even a fragment of the great wandering tale, which, in this chapter, may be said to break off short rather than terminate. Lately you caught me abjuring prefaces; but now I am led irresistibly into this one by a desire not to do wrong to the memory of those splendid fellows who, when I lay impotent, descended into the Jordan Valley and did battle there.

Those who lost their lives—and there are many of them—in the most terrible experience the battalion ever went through will surely rise up and complain wailingly that I am making too much of minor affairs, allowing to fall into oblivion all that long after-agony, if I do not do this reverence to their *manes*. Poor ghosts! would I had descended with you, a sharer in your torments; and you too, you few survivors, what would I not have given to have borne you company? Cannot one of you even now give tongue, and complete for the wonder of our children these records of the past?

★★★★★★★★★★

No signs of sluggishness or boredom marked the demeanour of the men as they trod the descending road whose amazing series of hairpin bends surely at last would carry them to Jerusalem. Now the guard-house was reached, and now the road doubled again and we saw that we were approaching a small village, the village of Kulonieh. A few hundred yards further on the road swept round to the north, and anxiously consulted maps told us that it would hold that course for about a mile before it gradually turned south-east and passed, with the usual variety of bends and turns in long descent, through Lifta to Jerusalem. The total distance of the journey would be about five miles. But no one knew how far our troops had advanced or how the matter stood.

The fog of war, an expressive phrase which cannot mean very much to those who have not been in it, had closed down almost completely upon this theatre, and though momentous events had happened, or were perhaps still in progress within a few miles of us, we knew nothing about them, and so were unable to orientate ourselves, or take our mental bearings. Trench warfare has its lulls and its suspenses, but they fall after a time into marked periods; in open or fluid warfare no one ever knows when we may be called on to take part in an attack. Anxiety, though danger may be far off, is always present, and officers are almost always in a condition of mental strain.

Even the men, marching along in the ranks, those happy-go-lucky fellows I always sympathized with and sometimes envied, felt something of the edge of immediate preparations, for there were few who were not specialists of one sort or another, with particular roles to assume when the emergency came. We were a harassed crowd, and though irresponsibility ran gaily over the surface. Duty, with a war-worn face, sat at her accustomed post. To be eager for news, and to know nothing; to be required to act in relation to events dimly conceived, and only half understood; to have to put forth your strength, physical and mental, for a race whose very length is unknown, is a squandering of effort, worse than that life of a suitor so bitterly described by Spenser.

Without the mental solace of fresh news, pressing forward to adventure and the unknown, we devoured the landscape, commenting

160

upon each triviality and variation of the slowly developing scene. We could not even guess what drama had been unfolding in the dragging night while in cold discomfort we had issued, bit by bit, our paltry rations.

Yet during those hours a tumultuous evacuation of Jerusalem was taking place, and midnight had seen the lonely governor of a city he was ceasing to rule savagely breaking up the instruments of his telegraph office with a hammer. The night had passed, he and the spectre of misrule had passed with it, and this sun, rising now to cheer us on our way, was shining too upon an informal ceremony at Lifta—a mile in front of us on this very road—where Izzet Bey's last legacy, his letter of surrender, was being handed over by a Turkish civil official. It was well, perhaps, that we did not know these things, for we might have fallen into a mood unduly sanguine, and been unbraced for the events that were to come.

We had scarcely passed the scattered stone houses that marked the beginning of Kulonieh, when the head of the column suddenly left the road and turned at right angles southward, in the very opposite direction to that we had expected to take. Most of the events of this wonderful day are clear and fresh in my memory, but a slight haze has gathered round these moments, and I cannot exactly call to mind the look of the piece of country where we turned off. It was a track that led downwards, I think between rough stone walls.

On the left, as we drew away from the road, in a partially enclosed field dotted with trees, the officers and some of the men of our field ambulance watched us go by. The colonel, who had been with the brigade ever since we left Salisbury Plain and now knew many of the officers personally, gave me a nod and a smile. This turning off the road, though the picture is smudged a little, has a peculiar interest for me now, and I find a dramatic value in it and the colonel's friendly recognition.

"You looked frightfully done up," he said afterwards. "I didn't think you were going to last."

These signals of distress, hoisted unawares, found no corresponding emblems in the mind. Tired and worn, like most of us, I felt that morning an exultant gladness, and strode up and down, shepherding my part of the column with a heart that leapt with excitement and sense of adventure. For now, the track had become a stony footpath, and we knew that we were descending into a wonderful gorge. Orchards lay at its wide entrance; already we were passing in amongst them; on either side the ground sloped upwards; we continued on our gradual descent. Trees were all about us, and our eyes, long accustomed to rocky summits, now fed delightedly upon patches of unexpected fertility.

The Bible country, someone remarked, was at last coming up to scratch. Everywhere little low walls, running up and down in the most haphazard fashion, divided the general sweep of trees and arable into what the parlance of our time would call holdings. The soil was still stony and of a reddish colour, but it showed occasionally promise of something richer. There were hints of that dark, fine mould, very fertile, always discoverable in volcanic regions. The morning was fine and clear, the air sharp and thin; Nature, fresh from her bath, seemed to have been born again.

The gorge was so closed in that we could not see the full extent of it, but felt rather than knew that on both sides of us, beyond the olives, were great upright cliffs of rock that held us as in the half-closed palm of a giant. Very little creatures we seemed to ourselves, hurrying in single file along the bottom. Presently the first halt came, and as we rested, the sun shot a few pale yellow shafts in on us, brightening everything and sending a gentle warmth. Enraptured at the strange beauty of the scene, and tuned up by the dry, bracing air, I turned to Temple and made some cheerful remark. But he was in a most unhappy frame of mind, shivering with cold and full of despondency.

"I wish we could go on again," he said; "the sooner we get out of this beastly place the better!"

Poor Temple! I can still see his white, unhappy face as he sat hunched up, shuddering, on a large stone.

The gorge was about two miles long, but our journey through it, if turns and twists are to be taken into account, must have been nearly double that distance. After a time, we crossed over the bed of a torrent, a mass of large white stones worn smooth by the passage of water, but now, to my amazement, dry. The thirsty soil of Palestine had sucked up all the rain fallen during the last three days: clearly there was still an enormous quantity to come.

For some time, we followed a narrow path, right up against the right-hand wall of the gorge; then it bent to the left, and the torrent, or *wadi*-bed, had to be crossed again. The pace was increasing. I was anxious not to lose touch with the company in front, for no one had any idea where the battalion was going; it was at these crossings, where the going was of special difficulty, that the men had to be hurried up, "boosted along," as we called it.

Jackson was doing his old turn, rounding up stragglers, giving an eye to the mules and to that epic steed, the famous "Marie Lloyd," my dear old ugly mare, who, bored and indifferent to the whole proceeding, her bones sticking through her skin, was being blithely lugged onward in the rear of everything by Henson, my rapscallion groom. Standing by the *wadi*-bed, I dealt with the men in turn, cheering and exhorting them, sometimes blaming, letting off small jokes, making facetious allusions to their known characteristics, all for the sole purpose of increasing the pace. At last, all but the stragglers were over, and I ran forward to see what was happening in front.

Across the *wadi*-bed the path we were following led upward, passing first through a small collection of trees. Here we rested, and when the report "all up" was received, started to tackle the ascent. This, at first, was trifling, but swiftly grew steeper, and before long we found ourselves hauling each other up over huge boulders of rock. How the mules were going to manage it I did not know, but looking down after some time I saw half a dozen of them collected on one of the hanging plots of land which generations of patient workers had made on the terraced end of the gorge, and being coaxed out of it one by one, preparative to being pushed, dragged, and any way urged upwards.

Three parts of the way up I met a woman and a child and a donkey, coming down. Luckily there was a space where they all could stand aside. She was of fine physique, upright, tall and handsome, a splendid peasant, and most picturesquely dressed. She wore a kind of bodice, and all the front of it was covered with raiment of needlework of various colours. After the natives of Egypt and the squalid women of the mud villages on the plains, with their filthy, matted hair and uncomely faces, and costumes like bundles of old rags, it was a pleasure to look upon this fine woman.

Later I met a man also good to the eyes, and of magnificent stature. These were Russian peasants of the colony of Ain Karim. A healthy, vigorous community, that had carved for itself out of a desert place a clean and beautiful habitation. An example for Jerusalem within a morning's march of her gates.

At length our climb was over and we stepped forth into one of the streets of Ain Karim itself. Part of the town to our right consisted of some fine buildings that showed up well against a mass of dark rock. In front of them the tall, plume-like trees that had attracted our attention from the hill of Kustul rose in stately fashion. I think they must have been cypresses. Here and there, wherever the ground permitted, garden beds of rich earth, as well looked after as if they had belonged to tome opulent English country-house, testified to the industry of this peace-loving people. To our left were several stone houses, perched upon the very brink of the gorge, and only reached from the road by flights of stone steps built over neatly turned arches. They were well proportioned, and the stone-work round their doorways was ornamented with various designs in colours.

I was more occupied in looking after my company than taking note of these matters, and it was only a few hasty glances I could bestow, as we hurried up the street and plunged into a confusion of passages. This was not a suitable occasion to reorganise, and I dared not stop, for I was hard upon the tail of the company in front and was afraid of losing sight of it.

So, on we streamed like ants, still climbing, for the passages ran upward, until at last we got free of them and broke out on to a hard road. This ran straight up for several hundred yards, where we could see that it turned round to the left, and doubled almost completely back upon itself at a higher level, still on the ascent. To the right of us, as we straggled up, there were more plots of cultivated ground, backed by rocks and a mass of hill.

The company in front was getting itself together, and further on I could see other companies, reformed and marching in a solid mass. Headquarters and the leading company had already turned the corner, and I was just falling into a pet with them for not halting, when at last they did. It was not long before we were all up and in column of route again. By the time the rest had closed the head of my company just reached the bend. Then we fell out and rested.

Small incidents of no real importance happening in the middle of a morning scene often stick in the memory when the chief actors in it are forgotten or have become shadowy. This is not merely a trick of the mind, but results naturally from known causes. These were the things we really delighted in or detested, these provoked the attraction or repulsion of our completest selves. The arrival of the general, the crash of the enemy aeroplane, though it might divert us mightily for the moment, made but a faint impression compared with affairs that affected us more intimately—the loss, say, of a pocket-knife when pocket-knives in reality held the stage.

So, without further apology I invite you to make a silent third as I share with my blue-eyed sergeant-major a tin of bully-beef. Of all the events of that vivid day none remains so brilliantly lighted in my mind. We were pleasantly warm now, almost hot, the corner of the road was sheltered, the sun shone brilliantly down. Was there, or wasn't there, time to consume it? No time to talk. He could do half, he said, and provide a biscuit.

It was a tin with a key on, and wonderful! it opened perfectly—no necessity to massacre it with brutal knife. The brand was right; I refuse to advertise it, but it was a name much sought amongst us. Bully-beef can be very good indeed, even when it is not dressed up to look like something else. Never have I so enjoyed so short a meal. The thin, keen air, the long climb, the early outset—these had hungered us; we devoured the food with a quick gusto that was almost beast-like. I tossed the tin away and looked round. The leading company was beginning to bestir itself. "Packs on," I cried to my own men, and then stuffed the last bit into my mouth. A moment later we were all busily getting into harness.

"All right, sergeant-major?"

"All ready, sir."

"Carry on!"

The company fell at once into its accustomed pace, rounded the bend, and began to take the ascent. For a few hundred yards the road ran straight, then turned to the right, and we saw before us a gradual incline. On the left the ground fell away, forming a great open depression, but on the upper slope of it several houses fringed the road with low-walled compounds beside them. On the right a mass of rock shut out all further view. For about a mile the road was clearly visible, running straight up; then it bent to the left, still apparently ascending, and seemed, finally, about half a mile further on, to pass over the long ridge that formed our skyline, and disappear near a small stone building.

We had not been long upon this road, and the most of the stretch remained for us, when the battalion came to a sudden halt, and we were ordered to get off it at once and pack ourselves, company by company, in the compounds. The rumour ran round that the halt would be a long one, but no one knew what would happen next. My compound, or stonewalled garden, was a tight squash for the company, and I had only just finished arranging the men in it, when the adjutant came up in a great hurry.

"Colonel's going up the road and wants all company commanders. He's got orders from the brigadier. You won't want your horse, he's walking. Can you come at once? Yes, it looks as if there's going to be a show. Do you know where Poy is? Over there. Thanks. Yes, I see him. See you later. So long."

Throwing a few words to the subalterns, I grabbed my Jerusalem map (the famous "Sheet Seventeen"') and set off. The colonel was waiting in the middle of the road, hitting himself with his riding-crop, a youthful figure full of nervous energy. He spoke as usual in his quick, nervy manner, letting off a succession of short sentences winged with schoolboy slang.

"Hullo, you all right? When's that fellow Poy coming? Shan't wait. Everyone else here? Damn the dust! Got all the men along? Don't know what's going to happen. All got maps, I suppose. Brigadier wants to attack. We'll go and have a look. All right. What a bloody day! Poy, you'll take the firing-line. That's for being late. Give C Company a rest. Come on. Time's short. Mac'll bring the battalion along."

At a tremendous speed, for the lithe figure, malaria-stricken and plagued with septic sores as it was, showed no signs of fatigue or waning energy, we all pounded up the long road as if we were in for a walking race. Halfway up on the right a shallow cave in the rock face was being used by the medical people as a temporary dressing station: someone was being bandaged as we passed. Not far from the cave the road was blown up, but it had been badly done, and guns had still sufficient room to get round the edge of the crater. The ground on the left was shaped something like the bowl of a big spoon; the road formed the right edge of it, and disappeared over the ridge at the top.

When at last, rather blown and very dusty, we arrived at the top bend, we carried straight on, clambering up the hill-side, which was covered with the usual litter of loose stones. We stopped a moment to get our breath, then grappled with the last slope. As we topped the crest, I was prepared to see the usual broken landscape of ravine and rocky mountain; instead, I had the surprise of my life, for there, straight in front of us, every detail clear in the brilliant sunlight, lay a walled city—Jerusalem.

We all gazed for a moment; then the colonel took up his tale.

"This place here—damn the wind—hold the map, someone—is the quarry. It's marked on the map 'quarry.' All see? Right-ho! Other brigade have had devil of a fight for it. Cleared off now up Nablus road. See Jerusalem? See trees left of the big wall—well left of that place like a convent. Poy, shut up talking; you'll have to advance over it in a moment, so you'd better listen. Does everybody see the tower? No, the little one, with a sort of belfry on it? That's what I call the convent. Right! Well, take that as our *right*; we shall push off from here—see? Make straight ahead. Then wheel quarter left. Sweeping movement. Then straight on. Right making for the trees. No one to enter Jerusalem. A and D firing-line; C and B support. A on the right. C support D. What shall we do then? Don't know. All quite clear!' "

Silence; then half a dozen questions, maps consulted and points identified. Meanwhile I, the left half of the supporting line, steadily and intently drank in the scene before me. The distance between us and the city was not less than two and a half miles. I have never seen anything so deceptive; it did not look more than a thousand yards at most. The intervening space consisted of an utterly bare desert of rocks, falling away from us to a slight rocky dip, then rising gradually to the very wall of Jerusalem.

No modern suburbs disfigured the city at this place, or, if some did, they were so few and insignificant that they are blotted from memory, but the city-wall was plain to see, bare as the rocky flats that ran up to it. In a kind of square people could be seen walking about; whether I saw them with glasses or with the naked eye, I know not, but I distinctly remember those moving figures. Three-quarters across, certain rocks had the look of fortifications.

In front of us was a system of trenches, and just beyond them the body of a man of our division was lying face downwards. I looked the scene over again and again, trying to memorise the principal buildings and think out a good description of the tower, some quick dodge to switch the subalterns on to it. A minute or two went by, and then we left the colonel and went pounding back to meet our companies.

Those unaccustomed to the irregularity of war, the turns and tricks, starts, surprises, and disappointments that are the very essence of its nature, will probably be a little dashed to learn that after all this bustle and preparation, the four companies were not, on their breathless arrival, hurled into action. The fog of war was still very thick in these parts, and I very much doubt if the brigade-commander himself could see more than a few yards ahead of him at this particular moment.

It was known that a brigade in front of us had swung north, but I believe it was uncertain whether the Turks in the meantime had come back round the corner, so to speak, for in the absence of the division that were coming up the Hebron road, but were now known to be late, it was impossible to make a clean job of squeezing the enemy out of Jerusalem, even though the city had been formally surrendered—a fact that had not yet penetrated to the troops.

We therefore lay in ignorance, disposed in four companies on the side of the hill and hidden from any enemy that might possibly be on the rocky plain; ready to advance at a moment's notice, and vexed at having been turned out of our warm resting-ground and precipitated up the road, to wait on an uncomfortable slope of rock in a strong, bitingly cold wind. Here we waited for some time. Nothing happened for a while, till the brigade-major was seen legging it up the hill and round the bend towards the small stone building at the top. He looked white and very tired, and limped. Shortly afterwards we were formed up on the road, marched up it to within about a hundred yards of the stone house, and told to sit down and be ready to move at any moment. Just before we moved, I met the colonel.

"Well," I said, "how about the attack?"

"It's a washout. General thinks the road's safe. We're going to march in as a brigade."

This seemed a very tame ending, but no one objected to a little more rest. The chief thing we were paying attention to was the wind, which, in spite of the bright sun, chilled us to the bone. Some of us on one side of the road and some on the other, squatting where opportunity offered, we waited the next turn of the wheel. On the left, close to where I was standing, a pile of booty tempted me sorely, but if it belonged to anyone, the brigade that had lately fought over this ground had prior claim to it, and I let it be. It consisted of all sorts of stuff, but my fancy was particularly taken with a large plate, of tinned copper, I think, dated 1636, and I had a hard struggle not to put it in one of my saddlebags.

I now remember that lower down the road I espied and put in my pocket a tennis ball, a most extraordinary thing to find in such a place. If we all came through this Jerusalem episode alive, this little ball, I thought, would give us a jolly game of rounders. life, like shot-silk, shimmers at every turn with unexpected colours, and even great historical happenings are full of holes and corners where things that do not matter sit innocently wagging their foolish tails. And there is laughter, which especially has a habit of coming to call upon me at awkward times, even though I tell Housekeeper Reason over and over again that I am not at home.

So, I shall never be able to write a good old thorough-paced tragedy, in the classic French manner, where nobody laughs or even makes a joke. But that very respectable battalion the Civil Service Rifles has just tramped by, and it looks as if we shall soon be moving. I must put an end to these reflections and warn the company. It is horrid to be caught napping.

The expected order was not long in coming; dreams and fancies gave place to action in the twinkling of an eye; a second twinkling saw us marching up the road in the direction of the stone house. That building had evidently had a bad quarter of an hour in the recent fighting; one of its sides was knocked out, and its roof, partly collapsed, lay at a rakish angle, just as if it had been sent us as a memento from the Western Front. Arms and equipment lay about; Johnny, who always fought like a tiger, had not given up that commanding ridge without a struggle.

And now we were coming to the beginning of the waste of rocks we had expected to advance over in extended order. The road ran right through it, like a white ribbon. Everything was absolutely bare. Just before the road flattened out on to the plain, at a place where a sloping plot of ground, buttressed up to form a garden, bounded it on the left and a ditch shut it in on the right, I noticed that the company in front, from which we had already lost distance, had checked, and was forming single file. I rode forward to see what the obstacle could be, and came upon a spectacle which, for tragic completeness, could not have been bettered.

Here were two guns of a Turkish field battery, hit fair and square by one of our shells, in the act of galloping away down the hill. Suddenly it had come to an end. The horses had leapt up and fallen sideways dead in their traces. In the ditch on the right a light ammunition wagon, evidently accompanying the battery, had been flung by its team to disaster. That the horses had taken fright was obvious, for a dead Turk lay in front of them, his hand still grasping the reins. Another Turk, horrible to look at, lay in the ditch. One of the gun limbers was burnt out.

It looked like an episode in a big battle-picture. The smell was sickening, but the sight of it as a spectacle of arrested movement superb. In the garden on the left a small group of wild-looking peasants watched us furtively as we circled round the guns. Something that one of them held glittered in the sun. It was a large crucifix, stolen or salvaged from some church. They completed the scene, the most perfectly disposed picture in real life I can ever hope to see. Months later I met a lieutenant in the Royal Air Force and described it to him. He showed extraordinary satisfaction.

"How splendid!" he said; "then they were guns, after all. I spotted them, you know, and everybody said it was transport."

The men were like babies as they passed these guns, staring about them instead of getting on with the business. I had a hard job to get the company clear, and by the time we were in column again, we had lost several hundreds of yards. The obstacle had had the effect of breaking the whole battalion up into companies, for headquarters always went pounding on on such occasions, anxious, I suppose, to keep up with the battalion in front. Brigade headquarters, tearing along in front of everything, did not condescend to think of such trivial matters, or perhaps had some urgent reason for being in such a hurry.

The march became a race, halts seemed to be forgotten, the men soon began to show signs of fatigue. Two nights with practically no sleep, and the long day behind us full of promises of excitement and yet empty of it, was beginning to tell on them, though all would have confessed readily that so far, we had done nothing. The road was never-ending: no one knew our destination, and no one cared. These men of mine always used to grin at me for talking about adventure, and were accustomed to remark that the only adventure they wanted was the return halves of their tickets—to London.

It seemed strange that we should be marching along a road which an hour or so ago had been considered dangerous, and have on our right the rocky plain over which we had intended to advance. The day—the great day—had been one long anticipation of something, we knew not what, that never seemed to come. There was not much left of it now, not many hours of sunshine before the cold night would have us in its grip. Surely this time we should reap the fruits of our long marching, not put up the bivouac tents, sleep, for once, in houses.

The part of Jerusalem which lay before our eyes and to which the road was taking us was its eastern suburbs, a mass of nondescript buildings, mostly of stone and flat-roofed in the Eastern manner, but varied by a few sloping expanses of red tile and disfigured in odd places by a patch or two of that enemy to the picturesque—corrugated iron. I have often consigned the inventor of it to perdition when, in pre-war days, I saw it in England replacing thatch or cobbling the roofs of pigsties, but during the war have become almost servile to my old enemy, even going to the length of hanging about in the moonlight in the hope of finding small pieces of him.

And now the shock to what I used to call my "artistic sense" was immediately followed by a fit of envy—how on earth had these wretched inhabiters of Jerusalem's outskirts got hold of it? Visions of a permanent mess roofed with it filled my mind; to us it was more precious than gold.

"Look," I said to the sergeant-major, who seemed in need of diversion. "See that little building over there? Corrugated iron. Good stuff."

"We could do with some of it, sir, if we settled down."

"Do you remember that lot we fetched from Arachli, in Macedonia?"

"When the men carried it on their heads over the mountains? You should hear them talk about it. Sergeant Bilkins was the great man on that stunt."

Reminiscence died down as we drew nearer and could observe the smallest details. There were people standing about at the point where the road passed in amongst the buildings. A house on the right a good deal larger than the others was decorated with several white flags. The men brisked up and became humorously appreciative.

"He ain't taking no chances."

"He's capitulated, that's what he's done."

"Finished the blooming war all on his own."

"'Fraid of us shooting him"—this from Jingle, a small, white-faced youth.

"Go on, you don't want to hurt nobody. Cup of tea's what you want."

Intense appreciation of this remark encouraged the happy inventor to continue:

"Look at those old chaps in dressing-gowns. Primitive, ain't they? Reg'lar old Shylocks. Dash me if some of 'em haven't got curls."

A few moments more, and we had passed the building that proclaimed so anxiously that resistance was over in this quarter, and were actually in a street that had houses on both sides of it. It was fringed, though not crowded, with as curious a collection of spectators as I have ever seen. I suppose "cosmopolitan" is the correct word, but it hardly does justice to the nondescript show that curiously watched our passage. Eastern for the most part and extremely dirty, it was variegated by numbers of persons of European origin, and by some who did not appear to belong to any nationality at all. There were brown people and white people and biscuit-coloured people. Some wore cloths over their heads and gowns with a girdle, others hats of a fashion ten years old and dirty-looking blouse and skirt costumes.

There was a strong flavour of Creole about the mixture: the people we had delivered, though picturesque, were certainly not "nice." Salutation was given in the various modes: some bowed low, some waved at us, some raised their hats. Some looked anything but pleasant: German landladies, perhaps, who were to reap a golden harvest by swindling officers in the months to come. But on the whole we were greeted with enthusiasm and an almost ridiculous deference, relieved by such remarks as "Hullo!" "All right!" and continuous demands for cigarettes.

After we had been marching for some hundreds of yards the column halted, and we sat down in the white dust against the walls of buildings. Brown bread was offered us, but at such an enormous price that hardly any one was able to buy. We were all very disgusted, for everyone was hungry, and we had not tasted a bit of bread for weeks. The halt lasted less than the usual ten minutes, and soon we were hurrying on again. This short rest did the men no good; the pace was too quick in front, and they began to straggle badly.

As we plunged deeper into the suburbs spectators became more numerous, till at last we were hemmed in on both sides, like troops in a London crowd. On such an occasion strict march discipline is absolutely necessary, or a company may quickly find itself broken up into small struggling groups. But the men were anything but smart, and looked anything but conquerors. Tired and jaded, the N.C.O.'s equally listless and by no means inclined to give orders, they plodded on anyhow with hanging heads, as if they were finishing the last lap of an exhausting item in a gymkhana programme. Their spirits, only an hour ago at the zenith, had dropped into their boots, and apparently, they were engaged in looking for them.

Ashamed and annoyed that, now of all times, they should appear to such disadvantage, I did what I could to buck up those immediately about me. It was with great relief that. Just as we were about to take a turning to the left, I saw that the crowd momentarily thickening at the corner was being taken in hand by a small body of men detailed for the purpose. We wheeled round, got clear, and found ourselves in a poorer but less crowded thoroughfare.

Jerusalem proper, the old city, now lay almost behind us, though we were unable to see anything but the immediate surroundings of the road along which we were passing. It was bordered by low, miserable-looking stone cottages, some of them half ruined. This quarter, I was afterwards told, was inhabited by poor Jews who lived chiefly upon charity. The road descended slightly, and it was not long before we came out into a large square, vaguely closed in by houses of all sizes. Once part of a rocky slope, the bare interior was still in its natural state, a rough table of slippery rock lying a-tilt.

The road bent round to the left to avoid these difficulties. But the company in front of mine was taking a bee-line for where it disappeared between the houses at the further end, and we began to struggle after them. Before we were half-way across the adjutant came up to me and whispered quickly:

"Get the men along as fast as you can, it's important. Don't know anything yet."

"Right-ho!" I said; "do what I can," and concocting a little tale, dashed back along the column and poured it into the ears of officers and sergeants. I said that important events might shortly take place, and that the general wanted to get the brigade clear of the square.

The effect was wonderful. The company, which had cut so poor a figure before the Jerusalem suburbans, smartened up and pulled itself together at the hint of a job. The response was an intellectual one; we were a moving mind, subject, like an individual, to despair and depression, but endowed with extraordinary resilience, and capable of more than any of us could have told.

The sections of fours straightened up, blank files obliterated by careless marching became again beautifully blank, sergeants remembered for a passing moment that they were wearing stripes. We conquered the square easily. The street swallowed us. We were going none knew where, but something was afoot. Sense of adventure, dormant for a while within me, woke up again, bringing with it the old feeling of nervous excitement. Nor did a sudden and totally unexpected halt, communicated from the front, altogether allay the feeling.

2: THE UNEXPECTED HAPPENS

The halt took place when we were in a short length of street, cut off somehow from the company in front, which had already turned the corner, but still in contact with the remainder of the battalion, which was just clearing the square. This street was wide enough to allow several sellers of nuts and figs and oranges to carry on their trade left of us, while to our right there was a pavement, fronting some kind of *café* or lodging-house. At first, we thought this was only a minor check—troops in front going through a narrow passage, perhaps— then I told the men they could sit down.

At once one of those situations arose which, calling for strength of mind and wise leadership, try officers to the utmost. We were all hungry, the men, the N.C.O.'s, my two subalterns, myself. Moreover, we had not had a chance of buying food for weeks, and here was some displayed before our eyes, with the prospect of more in the houses. Probably the inn would sell us a few loaves of bread. It was in my power to forbid it to the men but reserve it for the officers. A dirty trick; no, I would do nothing of the kind.

Yet if the subalterns were not to be allowed in, neither could the men be. And yet there was almost certainly bread to be obtained in such a place. Even as I was deliberating a little deputation came towards me, two platoon sergeants and my two officers. The usual request, so easy to ask, so hard to answer—might the men fall out?

"Why?" I asked, to gain time for thought.

"To buy things."

"I don't like it. Yes, I know they're tired and hungry, and all that, but I won't risk it. I can't."

"The other company is ——"

"'I don't care a damn what the other company is doing."

They were going away disappointed to join the murmuring throng—my grousing, discontented "Children of Israel"—when for sheer pity of them I relented and called them back.

"The men can fall out and buy what they want, but they are not to enter any houses—certainly not that inn—and they must come back immediately on a given order. And, look here, they're to keep control of themselves—I won't have any scrambling."

Grateful thanks followed. I snuffed the usual incense burnt at the foot of an indiscretion. The joyful news was communicated to the "children," who, without losing any time in admiration of their easygoing captain, spread themselves about the street, and tumultuously besieged certain old gentlemen in long robes, whose dry hearts were pulsing with excitement at the thought of our *piastres*. But outwardly they were still languid, almost deprecating.

Hungry and faint myself, but wishing to remain absolutely neutral, in order to be able to act with increased authority, if occasion should arise, I stood alone, regretting what I had done, and wondering when to shut it down.

At this moment the adjutant came up. I greeted him: Well, what's happening?"

Nothing. Outpost position later on. Other battalions are going forward. Shan't billet in Jerusalem I'm afraid. Look here: I'm busy, I shan't get a chance; get me some bread, there's a good fellow." And he produced what had come to be a great rarity—a twenty-*piastre* piece.

"All right," I said reluctantly, "but I'm not thinking about bread just now. When are we likely to move?"

"Don't know. Colonel doesn't know. Nobody knows," and he was off.

I slipped the coin into my pocket. I had made up my mind. All that buying would have to be put an end to. I would find some quiet, shopless street nearby, form up the company, and march into it. Then I should have them safe, and be ready for anything. They could grouse as much as they liked, but I had had them in tow now for two years, dragged them through France, cursed them up and down in Macedonia, jumped upon them properly during the months of training in Palestine. What a rotten thing to let the colonel down just for the sake of a handful or two of nuts and a few oranges! I had stood a certain amount of unpopularity and a small quantity of secret hate, but these fellows of mine were sensible enough really, if they would only think. I sent for Temple and told him to take over for a few moments. I would be back in five minutes.

It lay just round the corner to the right, the very street I wished for; straight, quiet, empty of people, without a single shop in it. I hurried back again, and called for Jackson and the sergeant-major.

"Look here," I said, "I don't like this. I'm afraid the men will get a bit out of hand. They don't mean anything, but some of the N.C.O.'s are so silly. And I'm nervous. I've got that peculiar feeling I had on the Vardar, the night we were bombarded and Mr. Trobus got into a mess with his patrol. All rot, probably, but I generally know, you know. Sort of second-sight. Horrid. Besides, I'm not taking risks. Not these sort, when anything's on, or might be. Cut it short; all this has got to shut down. See! I've found a splendid place round the corner. Dull as ditchwater. Henson, get ready to take 'Marie.' All right. Fall the men in. We'll go off straight away."

There was a good deal of grumbling and several N.C.O.'s had to be ticked off privately. Bilkins, the immortal Bilkins, comic genius of the company, was the naughtiest. He had to be looked for, and was found in a neighbouring street, buying bread. Be this recorded to his discredit. A boy he was, wearing a sergeant's coat. Really, after all these years, Bilkins!

Five minutes later the company was standing in the quiet street, facing in the proper direction, all covered off, once more a fighting unit. Then I made it my last speech.

"Company. Pay attention. You can take your packs off and sit on them. No one is to leave the ranks. I don't know what's up, and I'm going to find out. In five minutes, you may be in the middle of a battle. Or you may not. Point is, you are ready for it. Not going to be let down now. All right. You may smoke. Sergeant-major, I want two scouts."

It was not long before a little Welsh schoolmaster appeared, with another man, who is forgotten. Williams, as he is called here, was as eager as ever for excitement: his eyes shone with intellectual glee.

"Take off your packs, both of you," I said, "buckle them together, and sling them over 'Marie Lloyd!' You scouts always lose your packs on these occasions. It's rotten luck, but you shan't lose them this time. It's quite probable that I shan't want you, but if I do . . . well, that'll keep. I'm off to see the colonel."

Turning to the right at the bottom of the street, I hurried on, looking right and left, but seeing no one. Suddenly I ran straight into the brigade commander. This was a most unexpected meeting, and I blurted out what lay at the top of my mind:

"Looking for the C.O., sir—have you seen him?"

I don't know how much he thought I knew about the situation, or how much he knew about it, but he seemed to be in a desperate hurry. Nevertheless, to my great surprise, he stopped at once, and turned round.

"Come on," he said, "he wants you; you'll find him at the end of that passage. Goodbye." and he was off.

The passage was a narrow road, just wide enough to let troops down it, marching in fours. It was melancholy-looking and dilapidated. As I got to the other end of it, I saw that the houses stopped and there was a great view before me. But I had no time to look at views, for just outside, on the left, their backs to the wall of a house, were the C.O. and the adjutant. Signallers and the rest of headquarters lay up against the left-hand wall of the same house, but in the shelter of the passage.

"Hullo," said the colonel, "you're the very man I want. Order of attack as before. A and D will form the firing-line, C and B support. You'll support D. Damn and blast these Turks! Why the hell do they want to come back again this time of night? Dark soon. Are you ready?"

"Absolutely, if you will give me an objective."

"Well, look here. Do you see the hill? There's only one, damn it. See the trees on the right? Dark stuff, anyway. See little house, hut, chapel, meetinghouse, anything you like, on left? Very well. That's our frontage. You're on the left."

"From left hut to what looks like a stone gate-post in the centre. Will that do?"

"Gate-post? Yes. See what you mean. All right:"

"Where are the Turks?"

"How the devil should I know? Here, look out, keep against the wall. On the hill, I expect, damn them! Brigadier doesn't know any more than we do. Best of the brigade's on the left."

I hurried back, delighted at the thought of the company, all so snug and ready. But before I went, I had a quick look at the country. The rocks fell away from where we were standing, but there was a bit of a road through them. This wandered down what looked like a piece of Jerusalem that had grown up by itself. It lay in a hollow, bang in the way of the advance. There was a substantial house surrounded by trees, several smaller houses, and a regular mess of stone walls. Then came a plateau of rocks, all jumbled up. The ground then, as far as I could see, fell gradually into a valley, the bottom not visible, and then sloped right up into a great ridge of rocks and earth, whose top formed the horizon. A portion of this ridge, I learnt later, was the Mount of Olives.

Before long I was back amongst my own men. Now that we really were going to have a show it would not do to appear to be excited. Quickly, quietly, with a secret joy, I gave my orders. The simple words came out automatically:

"Rise. Packs on. We're in for a show. Officers and platoon sergeants." Then, in a lower voice, "You scouts ready?"

In two minutes, we were moving forward. On the way I explained what was happening.

"The first job," I said, "is to get past the village, round it or through it. I shall go down by platoons, at irregular intervals at the double, in the order in which you now are."

I halted the company three parts down the passage, and hurried forward with the two scouts. "That's the place," I said; "find out which is the best way, through it or round which flank. Come back at once. Meet us as we come out."

They doubled down the slope and disappeared. I brought the officers up and explained the situation, but my short conversation with them only momentarily diverted my thoughts from the main problem—how to get through the village. Gazing at it, I strained forward mentally into the unknown. Why not go to the right of it, round those houses? Then we should find ourselves on that ribbon of road, the white streak that ran into it at an angle, bent left, and passed out of sight.

So plain a road was an obvious target, "taped" to a certainty. Why, then, not try the other side? But that would be a long detour and take us clean off our frontage. Then we should have to go bang through. But perhaps there wasn't a way. How about getting the Lewis guns off the mules? We should have to find a place for them. O, chuck it all up and wait the event. And yet the brain began again: perhaps that little passage . . .

Necessity for action mercifully cut short this period of doubt and groping. The other company had gone. We were out of touch, how, I know not, in a moment. It plunged forward, by platoons, I think, and was swallowed up. It is necessary to impress upon the mind of anyone who has not experienced open warfare the way in which not only companies, but battalions and brigades, disappear into nothing when they go into action.

The landscape is so huge in comparison with the few figures upon it; a few fields, a mass of rocks, a village, some trees, a valley—let your men run forward into such a picture and they are gone. Their clothing favours invisibility, the broken landscape furthers it, the men themselves work for it, but the main reason is the size of the stage upon which the little figures run and tumble.

A few moments, and we too were launched. "Everybody ready?" I asked. "Then come on." I led the first platoon, to which I had attached company headquarters. The stretcher-bearers had a free hand to go where they liked, except two who were to accompany headquarters. Each platoon had its own Lewis-gun mules. The famous "Marie Lloyd," led by Rifleman Henson, followed in rear of the little body of men of which for the purposes of direction I had taken temporary command.

We doubled down the slope most successfully, gained the first hollow, were already on the outskirts of the village. Here I became conscious of a number of things like hailstones, coming at a terrific speed horizontally and spattering the rocks. "Hullo," I thought, "bullets again; now we're in for it," and I shovelled my party up under a wall, and began to look about.

It was a minute or two before all the platoons arrived. No one, as far as I could see, had been hit. We were very lucky. I was determined to keep the men formed up as long as possible, and not until the last moment dilute them into lines of skirmishers, with the necessary accompaniment of weakened control. The result of my peering and prying was a decision to go straight through the village and then get into touch with the other company, which, I presumed, was by this time almost on the other side. In a hasty minute's talk with their commander, I had implored him to let me know what happened to him—to remember that we were there to support him—not to forget our existence.

Neglect to send back reports, even negative ones, of however simple a nature, has caused the failure of millions of attacks, ever since men organised themselves for battle. It is an error that is always being pointed out, and always committed. He promised. And that was the last I ever heard of it.

Just as we were starting for our second bound, Williams, the scout, came running towards me.

"I'm going straight through," I said. "Will it be all right?"

He answered "Yes," and as we forged on, gave me a breathless description of what he had seen. The road, taking a great sweep, passed right in front of the houses, and we should have to cross it. He had seen nothing of the other company; it had disappeared. The Turks held the ridge, and were sweeping the approaches to it with machine guns. Down in the big valley-dip we should find cover. It would not be difficult to get through the houses.

A scramble, some twists and turns safely navigated, and we were at the entrance of a narrow way that ran between two buildings. There were no gardens or enclosures here; all was clear and open. The house to the left of us fell back a little way in the centre, forming a sheltered square, the very place for the Lewis-gun mules. I stationed a man to turn them all into it, as each platoon came up, and, while the first platoon was getting its guns, ventured with Williams along the passage.

It was very short, almost painfully so, and in less than half a minute we found ourselves in an irregular-shaped enclosure, bounded by strong stone walls about five feet high. Choked up in places with odd lumps of stone and covered with white dust, it served as a garden or front yard to the two houses, keeping them private from the highroad, which they overlooked. The wall had no gate in it. We should have to get over. The enclosure, at a pinch, could hold a company. Beyond the road was a bare plateau of jumbled rock, tipped slightly towards the enemy.

It seemed as if the men would never get those mules unloaded, but I believe the work was carried out with great rapidity. I now separated my headquarters from the leading platoon, pointed out a part of the plateau that looked as if it would afford cover, and told the platoons to get to it. I went third with my oddments—signallers, runners, and the like. We almost fell over the wall in our eagerness to put the road behind us, and then raced forward among the rocks, going like animals from cover to cover. Immediately we broke a fresh consignment of bullets pinged over us or spattered on the rocks. Still, nobody was hit.

We were now in a very awkward position, and it was not easy to decide what to do. The platoons were all intact, but had gone to earth at some little distance from each other, and to communicate with them was extremely difficult. It was certain that we had been marked down. Moreover, I could not at first see any signs of the leading company. At length I made out, on the hillside across the dip, a line of dark things, lying quite still, apparently a platoon in extended order. I waited to see what they would do. They did nothing. Williams now came back from a small scouting expedition, and reported that there was no one in front of us at all. I had another look at the hillside, and discovered that the supposed platoon was a series of little heaps of dark earth, deposited there, no doubt, by workmen.

Exasperated at my mistake and at having been held up by nothing, I decided to go straight ahead and take the ridge. The first step was to get over the plateau with the loss of as few lives as possible, and so down into the dip. There we could reorganise, extend, and begin the final stage. But first of all, I wrote a short message to the colonel and sent Williams back with it. It was to the effect that I could see no company in front of me, and was going to press the attack on my own account. Then followed a most anxious period, the getting my intention made known to the other platoons. Two of them I managed to visit personally.

It was difficult to remember where each was, and which was which. Nor could I see any one on my right or left; of attackers or of supporters there were absolutely no signs. My group of men was some little way in front of the others, and just as I was about to make a dash for the dip, a man, apparently belonging to another company, came running across our front in my direction. Twenty yards away, he sprang in the air, and at the same instant I saw in the middle of his forehead a red spot like the bud of a little rose. Then he fell dead.

I knew he was dead. If any man was killed instantaneously that man was. And though I was used to such things, the death of this fellow filled me with a sense of tragedy. My blood was not up. I was simply looking on. Just now he had been running along. And now two stretcher-bearers came up and began fiddling about with him.

Why couldn't they let it alone? The thing was done. He was dead. "Go away," I shouted. "Do something else. He's dead. I saw it. Go away."

Here was someone coming from another direction, from the left this time, wandering about. "Hi, there! get down, you fool; who are you? Good heavens!" It was a sergeant of the attacking company, acting sergeant-major, wasn't he, but why wandering here? It looked like a disaster. I didn't want him here, or any of his brood. Let them all get out of the light. But he had information.

"Where's your company?" I shouted at him. "Get down, get down!"

"O," he said, "is that you, sir? The company? It's gone, it's split up. Over there on the left. Dotted about that hill. What there is of it."

"Look here," I shouted back, "I'll tell you what to do" (for I wanted to get rid of him). "You double as fast as you can half-right, and get down into the dip. I'm coming too in a moment. Off you go."

To my relief he went, taking two or three other fellows with him. "The remains of company headquarters," I thought. "Thank the Lord they're clear of us."

Then passing the word round, we all got ready to leap, and up we leapt. Over the rocks helter-skelter, but not too fast, or we should straggle out and make a bigger target. Our dash took the defenders by surprise: they fired too late. Already we were in the valley.

It was not long before I had them all there and was busy reorganising. I would take the front line, with Temple—the survivor to carry on. The second and supporting line fell to the command of Jackson. Thus, we all had a look in. It was all against "Infantry Training": the commander ought to have brought up the reserve, flinging it in at the critical moment; but here we were playing a blunt game and had no use for the proprieties. I liked leading, and the men liked being led, and I wanted to see what the top of the ridge was like, and settle this cursed affair one way or the other and make an end of it.

We had almost got over the slightly rising ground at the bottom, when someone came staggering towards us, his hand pressed to his side. It was one of the officers of the attacking company, badly hit. I couldn't stop, but I shouted: "Get to the culvert if you can, down at the bottom of the dip. The stretcher-bearers are there." Then to myself: "Poor Tidcome! I hope he'll get there. Curse these infernal Turks!"

Then my mind swung back to the advance. Now we were passing the mounds of earth that had deceived me so badly. Now we were searching the upper slopes: in three minutes we should be on the top. What then? What waited us there? The firing had ceased. The hillside was so formed that we had been under cover the whole way. Were they then reserving their fire, or had they bolted at the last moment? What should we do when we got there? One quick glance, before my line of men arrived, would tell me everything. Thirty yards higher up, just where the ground curved over to form the summit, lay a big mound of earth and stones. O, if I could get a look round from the top of it.

"Yes, and then fall dead," said a prudent voice within me. Emotions swept pros and cons—the mind's swift rapier-play—clean on one side. I ran forward, my heart thumping like a hammer, and mounted to the top. It was the greatest deliberate risk I had ever taken. I stood straight up and looked swiftly round. Nobody fired a shot.

The glance just gave me time to decide what to do, when the attacking line came pressing forward over the top. I was standing exactly in front of the stone gateway I had agreed with the colonel should form the right of my objective. I had kept it steadily in view during our rush across the plateau, but during our advance up the hill we had evidently edged away too much to the right. It proved simply to be an unusually elaborate entrance into a stone enclosure, and on either side of it there were walls. The top of the hill was flattish, a mass of irregularly shaped upland holdings, white with chalk. Left and right ran a road.

The view in front was bounded by the slope of the ground, which, after keeping fairly level for about fifty yards, fell out of sight. That we were very high up was certain. The road in front of me ran along the top of the ridge to our right for about two hundred yards, where it turned to the left and disappeared. At the corner was a house of white stone, the only building visible. Casting your eye along the ridge from the gateway in front of us to the stone house, you would notice first a short stretch of wall, then a gap where a track-way passed over the hill, then more stone wall, bordering the left of the road almost up to the house. I do not pretend that I took all this in at a glance. I saw only the road and the stone gateway with the sheltering bits of wall on either side of it.

Immediately the men arrived, I shouted to them to take cover behind the walls. I was very suspicious. It was a rum start, coming up here after all that firing and finding nobody. The men, who were as active as squirrels and had thrown fatigue ten thousand miles away, twigged what I wanted straight off, and fled up to the walls like bits of iron seeking the magnet. Before half of them were there, I gathered up a dozen or so, rushed into the enclosure, and lined its further wall. Here a sight revealed itself. Before us lay an enormous valley, a great, deep hollow, set amongst a mass of hills and mountains. Peak upon peak, height after height, stretched far away into the distance.

But our devouring eyes were fixed upon a number of figures in the valley itself, men in groups and straggling lines. A great disappointment came over me. "Are they, could they be, the attacking party?" Were we then out of it, wretched tailors in the rear, men whom I had held in leash at the sight of a line of dark earth-mounds? Had the battle moved on into the valley?

Then a second thought came quick upon the first and throttled it. That company of ours was not wearing great-coats, and all those figures were coated. I looked again; yes, all of them. Why, then, they must be the Turks, those scoundrels who had just been potting at us. I danced with excitement, and, almost inarticulate with sheer joy, yelled for a Lewis gun. The men took it up. "There they are!" they shouted to each other. "The devils. Let 'em have it."

The first gun opened: a joyous little snapping sound of bursts. A squad followed, leaning on the wall: more men hurried up. There was a building on the left of the valley, where it bent round and ran away, perched on the steep side of it, and there was a doorway, and a path leading up to it.

Even as I looked, three men rushed into it. At once I turned the Lewis gun on. More men went through. We missed them, hitting the stone post on the right. I was wild with vexation. "Steady," I said, "for Heaven's sake, steady! You'll never get a chance like this again."

Then suddenly I grew wary and thoughtful, and the question of unprotected flanks came into my mind. Leaving Temple to run the merry game of Turk-potting, I sent Jackson with his own platoon to line a wall that ran on the further side of the track. This covered our right, and brought fire to bear on to a plantation of dark trees that grew on a kind of promontory at the back of the white house.

My left seemed safer, but I detailed a gun to watch it, and sent a runner in that direction, to get into touch with the rest of the brigade. The whereabouts of the remaining companies of our own battalion was still a mystery. I was just wondering whether I should send a platoon down into the valley with fixed bayonets (I had forgotten to fix them coming up the hill), when a well-known, matter-of-fact voice at my elbow, said:

"Hullo! By gad! You've taken the whole bloody hill!"

183

It was our sporting young colonel, the last person I had expected, though he never could stay out of a fight. We flung information at each other, and I said:

"Look here, sir: let me take half the company into the valley and hurry up those Turks."

"Damned if you do," said he. "Don't be a bloody fool!"

"Where's the rest of the battalion?" I asked. "I hope you got my message?"

"Other support company's right away back. They're coming along. Devil only knows where the attackers have got to."

"Where's Poy?"

"He's somewhere over on the right. Nobody's seen him. I say, how about that white house! Anybody been up that way yet?"

"No," I answered. "We haven't. Good stunt. I'll take a platoon."

"No, you won't. Let another fellow have a go. Send Jackson. Can you scratch a platoon together?"

"Platoon," I answered proudly; "ra-ther! I've got the whole boiling here. All properly organised."

"All right. Don't shout about it. I stop here for a bit. You go and ginger up old Jackson."

I ran off, and before many minutes a platoon, with Jackson at their head, was stealthily advancing in single file along the wall towards the house. I replaced by others the men I had taken away, and went back to find the colonel.

We were just discussing the advisability of sending another runner to work along the road to the left, when an outburst of fire came from the direction of the white house. We watched and waited. It grew more and more furious.

"Look here," I said at last, "I can't stand this. Let me take half a platoon up there and a Lewis gun, and see what's going on. I'm afraid Jackson must have got into a mess."

"Very well," he said, "but for God's sake be careful. And send back if you want any assistance."

I got my men together, and off we went along the left edge of the road. Light guns which earlier in the afternoon had been attached to the brigade were now putting shells over into the valley. They had come into action in the big square in the suburbs of Jerusalem—the square we had entered so wearily not very long ago. But I hardly heard them as we stole on like cats, wondering what we should bump into at the other end. As we approached the firing seemed to increase. At

ALL THE BUILDINGS—ALL THE TOWERS AND DOMES

last, we were near the house. Here against the wall, with a Lewis gun and one or two men, was the acting sergeant-major, the little man who had wandered up to me on the platform. Up against the wall, too, were other men, not of my company.

Jackson was nowhere to be seen. He was, they said, in the house. I could not make out where the noise came from until I noticed, on the other side of the road, lying at right angles to it, about fifteen men, their rifles stuck over a kind of emplacement, firing away like madmen. Bullets were hitting the rocks all round them, sweeping the road, and occasionally flirting against the wall of the house. I ran across the road. As I did so a tall N.C.O. made as if to cross in my direction. Almost as we met, he fell dead, shot through the throat. I went up to the men and lay down beside them.

"Cease fire!" I shouted. "What's your target?"

"They're firing at us," said one of the men.

"What's your target?" I repeated.

"Them houses."

I looked, and saw a majestic scene in front of me. To my right Jerusalem. All the buildings. All the towers and domes. To my left, where the road bent down the hill, rose, quite near us, from the left of the road itself, the great stone shaft of the famous German Hospice, that for height outdoes everything in the neighbourhood and is a landmark for miles.

"It's absolutely useless," I said, "blazing away at Jerusalem like this. You're only drawing fire. Shut it down at once and take cover. One man keep a lookout."

They cooled down after this. Then, crossing the road again, I ran into Jackson. He was very excited. He had one view of the situation, and I had another. Neither of us had time properly to explain his own. But I didn't want explanations. I simply desired to know if he had cleared the house. And I asked him point-blank.

"I say, look out," he said. "For Heaven's sake, look out. Yes, I've been into the house."

A bullet hit the window behind us. It looked as if someone was firing from inside.

"Can you," I said, "send a message to the colonel to say it is cleared?"

"I can't do that."

"Then go in again, and come back when you can. We *must* clear it. I dare say it's all right now, but we must know for certain. I'm going to wait here with a Lewis gun. If you want me, send a man. Then

186

I'll bring up the gun and some men. I've stopped those fools over the road from firing. Turks are in the Hospice, I believe. That beastly division on our right has let us in for this."

He dived into a doorway that lay at right-angles to our protecting wall—a doorway that led into a yard at the side of the house. It was not very long before a man appeared.

"Lewis gun wanted, sir."

"Right-ho!" I said, and very cautiously we all advanced.

First, I poked its nose round the corner. Then we got into the yard. Outhouses with doors to them opened into it. Hurriedly I went through them, one after the other. "All clear," I remarked. "Take the gun into the garden."

They disappeared and I made my way round to the back. The light was beginning to fade, though I hardly noticed it. But I could see, over my left shoulder, an enormous mass of black cloud coming down upon us from the north. I was now in a garden. In front and to the right were trees, the beginning of the plantation I had previously seen from afar. A splendid place, I thought, to direct operations from. The flank attack did not worry me, for the nature of the ground made it impossible for anything serious to develop; moreover, I had plenty of men. But I was anxious about that copse. In a few minutes Jackson came running back.

"We've got 'em, we've got 'em! They're running away. Where's that gun!"

"I've sent it up. And look here. Is this house all right?"

"Quite."

"Searched the roof?"

"Didn't think of it. I'll send up some men."

"Do. And——" *Crash!* Something unseen came out of the air and dealt me a tremendous blow.

A great wonder seized me. Then, as I fell, full consciousness of what had happened dawned in my mind.

"Damn it!" I said angrily. "Hit. The devils!"

My blood was hot. Vigour had not yet left me.

"All right," said Jackson tremulously; "it's in the arm."

"No," I answered, growing weaker even as I spoke. "It's not. I'm done in. Go back and look after that gun. It's an order. Go."

A chill wind was blowing. The sun was hid. Darkness was coming on. It grew colder and colder. A sea of ice flowed into my body. I closed my eyes. Then I heard voices.

"O, I say, look 'ere! 'Ere's the capting. You catch 'old of 'im this side, Egan. 'E's cold. Take off your coat. 'Ere, come along, Brewer. This won't do. You stay 'ere while I look about for a stretcher."

It was Thunder & Co., the men who were always giving me trouble. Slowly, carefully, with infinite patience, exhorting each other in their Cockney dialect, cursing and swearing, even quarrelling, the gang bore me away. Over the stones, bump, bump, bump, wandering, wandering. Night and the chill rain shuts the picture out. Night on the Mount of Olives. Misery and labour untold lay in her womb, misery and bitter cold for the tired men and officers whom outpost duty claimed. But the tale must falter and die, for the adventures of its narrator are ended.

The Taking of Jerusalem

By Edmund Dane

Both the railway and the road routes between Gaza and Jerusalem had been cut, the divided fragments of the enemy forces could not reunite save well to the north. On the British side, to emphasise this striking military advantage had become the primary aim.

The nearest point at which possibly north of Gaza the enemy might attempt a stand was the Wadi Hesi, where another western spur of the main ridge came close to the coast, broken here by the inlet of the river. To this position the enemy had always attached a capital importance. In present circumstances it was of the utmost moment to him. Looked at broadly, the situation was this. One arm of the British pursuit was being pressed across country through Sheria towards the north-west; another was being pushed coastwise to the north.

Between the two arms, thus converging, was a large body of Turkish troops, the 26th Division, commanded by Fakr ed Din Bey, and the 54th Division, commanded by Nashui Bey. The problem was to get them out, and on either side, it was at the utmost a question of hours. Not the least notable feature of the matter is that the retreating were more numerous than the pursuing troops. It was not by weight of numbers that General Allenby had so far won; it was by skill in strategy, and by the able tactics of his lieutenants. Staggered the enemy had been, but he was by no means so weak as not to put up a stiff fight when cornered. And in the circumstances, seeing that so much was at stake, he did at both the points of pressure fight his hardest.

On the British side, the 52nd Division was pushed on to the Wadi Hesi forthwith. And here, though it was, relatively speaking, a minor affair, there was fought one of the most remarkable actions of the Great War. The 52nd Division found the spur beyond the River Hesi held by a strong Turkish rearguard. Undaunted by the hostile fire, the sturdy Lowlanders crossed the river and carried the height. Then the enemy rallied and the Scotsmen were pushed off the bluff on to its southern slope. Rallying there in turn they attacked a second time. Once more the Turks, beaten in the hand-to-hand encounter were driven off. More enemy forces were now, however, brought up, and another Turkish counter-attack, though at a heavy cost, won the hill. But the Lowlanders, at their old rallying point freshly supplied with ammunition, came on a third time and cast the foe out.

It was still not enough. With yet a further infusion of strength, the Turks attacked again and cleared the top of the bluff once more. Their triumph was transitory. Before they could establish themselves the Scots, rebounding, were into them with the bayonet, and they ran. Because it was called for in order to save the Turkish Army from irreparable wreck, there was a fourth counter-attack, and for the fourth time the position changed hands. But was this final? Not at all. The fifth appearance of the Lowlanders, coming on with a wild battle shout, was a climax which not even Turkish fanaticism or German fury could withstand. The Turkish morale gave way. The Lowlanders had been ordered to take this position, and they took it.

And this experience was paralleled by that of the 10th Division. In advancing towards Huj at the other point of the convergence, the Irishmen fought and defeated in succession three bodies of the hostile rearguard in a distance of ten miles, and within as many hours. These were the episodes which demoralised the Turkish Army.

The victory of the 52nd Division had opened up the Jaffa road, and mounted troops were pushed north along it. There were now two points at which chiefly enemy rear-guards were posted with orders to hold each to the last. One was at Beit Hanun, the junction north of Gaza of the Jaffa route with that from Jerusalem; the other was Huj.

Through Huj lay the line of retreat of those enemy forces who had been holding the Atawineh and Baha groups of defences. Gaza lost on the one side and the Ruweika and Rushdi defences on the other, they were left no choice but to hasten out. Evacuating their positions on the night of November 7, and moving by cross routes upon Huj, they had there posted their rearguard. The distance between Huj and Beit Hanun is not more than ten miles, and it was through that narrow gap that the retreating Turks had to make good their escape. It will be seen, therefore, how much depended upon these combats. The fighting at both points was stubborn.

At Beit Hanun a whole day was taken up before the rearguard was broken. At Huj the resistance was overcome by an intrepid charge of the Worcester and Warwick Yeomanry, who rounded up twelve of the enemy's guns. But the time taken up had been enough to allow the main body of the Turks to slip through. It was in that manner that the remains of the 26th and 54th Divisions got out. A mass of munitions and stores and much of their artillery, however, had to be abandoned.

From Huj the British pursuit was pressed towards El Meidel, Julis and Beit Duras; it swerved, that is to say, laterally towards the coast so as to take the Turks retreating north in flank. On the other wing, in the meantime, the enemy had fallen back from Tel Kuweilfe by cross routes towards Hebron. The difficulties in the way of the British movements were now less the strength of the opposition encountered than the problems of supplies and of water. Already the British troops were most of them a good many miles from railhead, and in a country little favourable for transport. Water there was and enough, but it had to be drawn up from wells, and even where the means for drawing it had not been destroyed, as was frequently the case, rapid distribution was not easy. To neglect these problems would in the end have meant loss of time, and it was important, if the enemy was not to rally, that time should be saved.

Even on November 9 evidences were not lacking of a reaction. The larger part of the broken Turkish Army was that retiring north. To relieve the pressure upon it the enemy was hurrying what reinforcements he could raise towards Hebron, and he made a counter-demonstration from that place. But General Allenby advisedly treated this apparent threat for what it was worth. He was aware that in the fighting round Tel Kuweilfe this smaller part of the Turkish Army had suffered severely. He knew it to be short alike of supplies and of ammunition, and its hasty retirement over indifferent roads and through difficult country had contributed further to its disorganisation. Effective counter-attack from that quarter was therefore not immediately to be looked for. He contented himself accordingly on that side and for the present with blocking the outlets, and pressed the main pursuit.

The effort of the enemy was now to form a new line extending from Hebron north-west through Beit Jibrin on the main road from Gaza to Jerusalem, and by that means to link up with the coastal force. As they moved forward the British found lines of freshly dug, but unfinished trenches.

This opposition rapidly stiffened. Indeed, it soon became apparent that the enemy had determined to make a stand. British movements were slower than hitherto not merely because of the supplies problem, but because of the temperature. There had set m from the southern deserts a hot wind which rendered marches fatiguing.

At once to flank the British movement along the coast, and to cover the routes inland to Jerusalem, the enemy had from Beit Jibrin northwards taken up a position along the western edge of the highlands as far as El Kubab on the Jaffa-Jerusalem road. It was a strong position, for it barred the defiles.

But as a menace it failed. The British mounted troops moving along the coastal plain continued to press north. Already on November 11 they had reached Nahr Sukeirer at the outlet of the Mema River, thirty miles north of Gaza, and secured a bridgehead on the farther side, the Murreh hill.

It was the intention of General Allenby to attack the right of the hostile front near the Jaffa-Jerusalem road; a bold decision, but one best calculated to embarrass and puzzle the enemy. If he moved the weight of his force to resist assault there, the Turkish general risked a rupture of his centre, and he had already experienced the peril of that manoeuvre. It was not probable, therefore, that he would run the risk a second time.

The attack, entrusted to the 52nd Division, supported on their right by the mounted troops, took place on November 13. Both infantry and cavalry had to advance across a rolling plain. Walled, flat-roofed villages surrounded by plantations afforded points of support for the defence. But the advance of the Lowlanders was intrepid, and the cavalry rode forward with conspicuous dash. The enemy's positions were reached and cleared, two of the villages he held, Katrah and El Mughar, wrested from him, and his front broken. The horse pushed in, took 1,100 prisoners, 3 guns, and numerous machine-guns.

This success enabled the British, while the pursuit to the north went on, to push the remainder of the Turks east and frustrated their attempted conjunction. So far, the effort to arrest the pursuit had broken down. The Turkish losses alike in artillery, munitions and other equipment and stores had been heavy. The 9,000 prisoners taken up to this time, and the enemy's casualties, though severe, might conceivably and possibly be made up. The disorganisation of equipment would take time, and much time, to repair. For the same reason as in Mesopotamia, even though it might not be to the same extent, the Turkish campaign in southern Syria had been seriously crippled.

One result of the victory of November 13 followed at once. On

November 14 the British troops reached and captured, together with a haul of rolling stock, the railway junction where the line from Gaza joined that from Jaffa. This was a vital link in the enemy's communications.

The pursuit north was pressed as well as the advance east. The cavalry reached Ramleh and Ludd, the former on the main road, the latter on the railway to Jaffa, and occupied both towns by the evening of November 15. By this move Jaffa had become undefendable. The port was occupied on November 16 without opposition.

This capture was important. In possession of Jaffa, the British Expeditionary Force had a new and excellently situated base for oversea supplies. The main handicap of the campaign had been overcome. (The transport of supplies by rail across Sinai was reduced from 2,000 tons to less than 900 tons a day.)

No feature of the operations up to this time had been more remarkable than their rapidity. A fortnight only had elapsed since the attack upon Beersheba, but in that fortnight, besides the destruction of the enemy's fortified front, there had taken place, reckoning from the British lines before Gaza to Jaffa, an advance covering 75 miles of country. Farther inland the advance had covered forty miles, and that in spite of the trying conditions of the climate and some stiff fighting.

All the southern part of the coastal plain had been cleared. Save, however, its southern extremity, the enemy still kept his footing on the highland ridge; the question now was to wrest it from him.

Advance from the plain through the minor defiles facing west was impracticable. The one break of any importance was that through which was carried the Jaffa-Jerusalem road, but even that defile was narrow and the enemy had not neglected to obstruct it.

Between Hebron and Jerusalem, the backbone of the uplands rises to more than 3,000 feet above sea level. There is a fall to 2,363 feet where the main road from Jaffa to Jerusalem crosses what is to all intents a broad pass, but beyond this again to the north the chine rises, attaining at its highest point an elevation of nearly 2,900 feet. As this part of the chine, known as the Nebi Samwal ridge, ran parallel with the Jerusalem–Nablus road, and as it appeared necessary to strike that road at some point north of the Holy City in order to ensure evacuation of the country to the south, the ridge had to be seized.

A movement by the yeomanry from Ramleh, through the hills eastward, was begun on November 17. Following secondary routes, they reached Shilta. There is a track from that place over the moun-

JAFFA

MEDITERRANEAN SEA

Ludd

Ramleh

Old Road

Defile

Saris PASS

Nebi Samwal

Kuret-el-Eneb

JERUSALEM

2540 FT.

The Ridge

Road to Nablus

Jericho

④

④

Junction Station

Main body of
Turks in Retreat

Bethlehem

2970 FT.

Main Road

The Chase

2929 FT.

Hebron

Smaller body
of Turks in
Retreat

DEAD SEA

GAZA

Wadi el Sheria

Sheria

TEL KUWEILFE PASS

Motor Road

1130 FT

1540 FT

⑤

Beersheba

R. Guzza

Rafa

Posts

Cultivated
Plain

El-Khalasa

Bir Aslug

SINAI   DESERT

Movement of British Forces - - - →
T.T. Turkish Defences
B.B. British Lines
② Tuweil-abu Jerwal Ridge
④ El Ruweika Defences
⑤ Turkish Line at battle of
      El Kubab

SCALE

0   5   10 MILES

tains, but it proved impassable for wheeled traffic. The move covered the flank of the advance through the main defile. The opposite flank to the south was similarly covered by an advance of the Australian Light Horse.

On November 19 the infantry set out. The opposition met with was from Turkish rear-guards. By the end of that day, however, the main defile had been cleared as far east as Saris at the western foot of the pass, where the elevation is 2,000 feet. Saris had been defended with some obstinacy. Many Turkish dead were found among the rocks. For both sides this mountain campaigning was toilsome work. To the burning *sirocco*, which sweeping over the country from the deserts had rendered the first days and, much more, the first nights of the pursuing movement oppressive, and, in a land where it was hard to obtain water enough, had tried the endurance of the British troops to the utmost, had now succeeded heavy and continuous rain accompanied by a change from heat to cold, sharpened here by the height above sea level.

At night the men rested where and as they could in the rain amid the vast boulders and rock fragments strewing this savage defile. Hard, indeed, are the labours of war, and if there is glory in it no small part of that glory, assuredly, is the discipline which can support hardships such as these, with patient cheerfulness and unabated courage. The truth is more impressive than fiction.

From Saris the summit of the pass is reached by a zigzag road, about two miles in length. The enemy was prepared to dispute the passage. He had a force of some 2,000 rifles with numerous machine-guns, and the village of Kuryet-el-Enab, which marks the summit, had been organised for defence

Early on November 20 the British troops resumed their attack, aided by an offensive movement along a secondary and nearly parallel road some miles to the north. It had been judged that to force the pass would prove a stiff if not a costly piece of work. A hostile force well-armed with machine-guns in a narrow defile should without too much difficulty render it impassable. Happily, however, there were two factors in the British favour. When morning broke the whole defile was enveloped in fog. It was one effect of the cold, and it neutralised probably nine-tenths of the enemy's advantage. In the circumstances the tactic adopted was an attack with the bayonet. The men stole forward noiselessly, at their head the Gurkhas and other Indian troops, adepts at mountain warfare. The practised skill of these men was the second favourable factor. How the fight was going those in the rear could not see, but presently through the mist rolled back the cheers of the attackers, mingled with the crackle of rifle shots, the rapping of machine-gun volleys, and shouts of anger or terror. But the cheers dominated all these sounds, and they were sure omens of victory. The Turks were driven out of Kuryet-el-Enab at the bayonet point. The attack to the north carried the village of Beit Dukka, and gained there a footing on the chine. To clear it the troops moved from Kuryet-el-Enab along the line of the backbone northwards. By nightfall the whole Nebi Samwal ridge had been won.

The yeomanry were now thrown forward to the east of the rise, but the enemy was plainly determined to keep the Nablus road open. He had received reinforcements, was well provided with artillery, and strong in machine-guns, and it was evident that a powerful effort would have to be made to dislodge him. Indeed, the first use made of his reinforcements had been to launch two counter-attacks with the object of recovering the chine. Owing to difficulties of transport, the British had at this time only a very limited artillery support. The counter-attacks were beaten, but until the guns could be brought forward, a further advance, it was manifest, could not be essayed. All that could be done in the meantime was to consolidate the positions gained.

Nevertheless, the rapidity of the British movements had realised results which General Allenby justly described as invaluable. They had penetrated the defiles before the enemy had had the opportunity to render them impassable. General Allenby observed:

"The narrow passes from the plain to the plateau of the Judean range, have seldom been forced, and have been fatal to many invading armies. Had the attempt not been made at once, or had it been pressed with less determination, the enemy would have had time to organise his defence in the passes, and the conquest of the plateau would then have been slow, costly, and precarious. As it was, positions had been won from which the final attack could be prepared and delivered with good prospects of success."

The enemy now resorted to the tactic of harassing local counter-attacks, carried out as far as possible by surprise. His chief efforts were still directed against the Nebi Samwal ridge. In these he incurred serious losses. The attacks proved consistently unsuccessful.

During this interval—the later part of November and the first days of December—the British were busy improving roads and tracks, and in moving forward supplies and guns.

The plan of the renewed operations was to combine the attack west of Jerusalem with an advance from the south through Hebron. Apparently on the part of the enemy the latter development, in effect a turning movement, had not been looked for on account of the rugged character of the country.

The column detailed for the purpose—the 53rd (Welsh) Division, and a regiment of cavalry—moved out from Beersheba on December 4. By nightfall on December 6 their vanguard, after an extraordinarily rugged and toilsome march, was ten miles north of Hebron, and some six miles distant from Jerusalem. The general combined attack had been fixed for the 8th, and the column from the south, having passed Bethlehem on the 7th, was intended to co-operate from positions three miles south of Jerusalem.

On December 7, however, the weather had broken. Rain fell heavily, veiling the whole of the uplands in mist, and so far, obscuring the roads that movement, and especially the movement of supplies, became next to and in some instances quite impracticable. The southern column was in consequence delayed.

But the western attack had achieved results of considerable importance. Difficult as the conditions were, the troops advanced over hilly country some four miles, captured the Turkish defences both west of Jerusalem and north of the city, and, seizing the Lifta Hill, carried the front forward to within one and a half miles of the city's western walls.

Next morning (December 8), continuing the attack, the 60th and 74th Divisions fought their way north of Jerusalem across the Nablus road. The most formidable of the hostile positions were some tiers of trenches on the farther side of the Wadi Surar, a depression having, as usual in Palestine, precipitous sides, and at Deir Yesin, on the west of Jerusalem, fortifications called by the troops the "Heart" and "Liver" redoubts. Despite rain and mist, the Wadi Surar trenches were taken, though it looked a feat bordering on the impossible, and both "Heart" and "Liver" were torn out of the defence.

At the same time, the Southern Column, which had occupied Bethlehem on the previous day, had moved to the east. In a dashing charge two battalions of Welshmen, with the Cheshires in support, had ousted the Turks from the Mount of Olives. By one of the strange vicissitudes of the war this ground of revered memories became the scene of a savage bayonet fight. The fight enabled the Southern Column to get astride the main road to Jericho. The Turks left in Jerusalem were now enclosed.

With the loss of their positions commanding the Wadi Surar went, in a military sense, and so far as Jerusalem was concerned, the Turks' last hope, and that at the Turco-German Headquarters was realised at once. From Constantinople the orders were to hold out to the last extremity. In accordance with them, Jemel Pasha telegraphed instructions to Izzet Bey, the Turkish Governor of Jerusalem, to evacuate the Jewish and Christian population. Izzet wired in reply that there were no vehicles to be had for helping the inhabitants to get away. Back came the order that the inhabitants in that case must leave on foot. Measures were therefore taken for a wholesale clearance.

The police were sent round to warn religious chiefs and other leading persons to be ready to depart forthwith. When the report of the intended deportation spread, as it did with the usual rapidity of bad tidings, the non-Turkish inhabitants, knowing well what it meant, hid themselves in every cellar and lurking place. Outside was the thunder of the battle, every hour drawing nearer and growing louder; within the ramparts was terror. This was the state of affairs on December 8. At sunset on that day, however, the rumour got abroad that the British could be seen from the city. Part of the 60th Division had then, in fact, stormed the Lifta position, and this fighting was in full view from the walls. While the excitement of these events was at its height, a Turkish transport column galloped furiously in, and thundered along the streets towards the Jericho exit.

In its wake came a panic-stricken rout of Turkish infantry, ragged, bootless, and beyond control. On sight of the flying transport, they had deserted the trenches *en masse*, and surged in by the gap in the western wall, throwing away their arms, struggling and fighting to get through first. Behind and among them were officers, some Turks, some Germans, shouting with rage; flogging the mutineers back; trying to force them to pick up abandoned rifles. The scene was pandemonium. Most, however, defied authority. By the non-Turkish inhabitants, the panic was welcomed as a sign of deliverance. Of the deportation no more was heard.

All that evening (December 8) the Turkish batteries west and south-west of the city were blazing away their last shells. But that this was the closing act in the four hundred years of Turkish rule became evident when Izzet Bey towards midnight went to the telegraph office, sent the staff about their business, and, it is recorded, himself set about smashing the instruments with a hammer. (*Official Record of the*

Egyptian Expeditionary Force.)

In the early hours of the morning the inhabitants from within their houses heard a steady, ceaseless, shuffling tramp. It went on hour after hour. It was the beaten army in retreat. By an interesting coincidence, the day was the Jewish Festival of the Hanukah, commemorating the deliverance of the city by Judas Maccabeus. Of the civil officials the last to depart was Izzet Bey. His final official act had been to write a letter of surrender, and send it to the mayor, with orders to deliver it to the British commander. That done, he availed himself—Turkish fashion—of a cart and team belonging to an American resident, Mr. Vesper—the only cart and horses left in Jerusalem which till then had escaped requisition. Izzet Bey evidently had had an eye to emergencies. He rode out along the road to Jericho.

For five hours the defeated troops, sullen and weary, had shambled across the city. At dawn on December 9, while the last stragglers were leaving to the north and east, the mayor came out at the western gap accompanied by two policemen, each carrying a white flag, and by a throng of inhabitants who on the departure of the Turks had issued from their hiding places. The mayor walked towards Lifta. In the British lines the impending surrender was already known, for rumour of it had been circulated beyond the walls. The mayor was taken to Headquarters of the 180th Brigade, and handed Izzet's letter to Brigadier-General Watson. Pending instructions, General Watson went back with the mayor, placed guards over the post office, in some of the hospitals, and at the Jaffa gate, and helped to re-establish public confidence.

As soon as the Turks had gone, and even before the last of them were out, crowds had stormed the Turkish barracks, and in revenge for repeated and severe requisitions, had looted them. The buildings were unroofed, doors and window frames torn out, and floorings carried away for firewood. When, however, the detachments of British infantry marched in, these disorders ceased. The capitulation was arranged with Major-General Shea.

General Allenby made his official entry on December 11. In his honour the Jaffa gate, long disused, was reopened. The general came in on foot, and the formalities were the simplest. They consisted of the reading in the English, French, Arabic, Greek, Italian, and Russian languages, from the entrance to the citadel below the Tower of David, of a proclamation that order would be maintained in all the holy places of the Jewish, Christian, and Mohammedan religions, which would be guarded and preserved for the free use of worshippers. After the proclamation, leading ecclesiastical and other notables were presented to the British commander. The presentations concluded, the general, again on foot, left by the Jaffa gate.

The feature of the proceedings was the crowd which witnessed them. There had been recalled in association with the event a curious Arab prediction that when the Nile flowed into Palestine a prophet from the West would drive the Turks out of Jerusalem. (*Official Record of the Egyptian Expeditionary Force.*) The Nile had flowed into Palestine, though through a pipe-line, and public desire to cast eyes on the "prophet" had prevailed even over the traditional fear inspired by the long Turkish suppression of all and every assembly. From beyond memory anything in the nature of a meeting had been dealt with by the Turks as criminal conspiracy, and with a severity knowing no limits. In spite of that, the whole population now turned out. They were not molested, and to them this was a wonder, which heightened the portent. Amid every sign of common emotion priests and others embraced each other. Some, it is recorded, shed tears of joy.

From the political viewpoint the British occupation of Jerusalem was an event of first-class importance. But from a military point of view, it should not be forgotten that the prestige of the Turks throughout the Near East has always been essentially that of arms. By the events of this signally brilliant campaign that prestige had been brought to a point beyond precedent low. Through defeat the vitality of a military dominion is irreparably impaired. Here was revealed the radical mistake of German "penetration." It had left the Turkish Empire unable to stand alone, yet had afforded no substitute efficient to sustain the Empire against attack.